W9-CBV-688

Taste of Home
Appetizers
& Small Plates

201 ENTICING IDEAS FOR PERFECT PARTIES

TASTE OF HOME BOOKS • RDA ENTHUSIAST BRANDS, LLC • MILWAUKEE, WI

Taste of Home

Reader digest

A TASTE OF HOME/READER'S DIGEST BOOK

©2015 RDA Enthusiast Brands, LLC, 1610 N. 2nd St., Suite 102, Milwaukee WI 53212-3906. All rights reserve◆
Taste of Home and Reader's Digest are registered trademarks of The Reader's Digest Association, Inc.

EDITORIAL

Editor-in-Chief: Catherine Cassidy
Creative Director: Howard Greenberg
Editorial Operations Director: Kerri Balliet

Managing Editor, Print & Digital Books:
Mark Hagen
Associate Creative Director: Edwin Robles Jr.

Editor: Amy Glander
Art Director: Maggie Conners
Layout Designer: Catherine Fletcher
Editorial Production Manager: Dena Ahlers
Copy Chief: Deb Warlaumont Mulvey
Copy Editor: Mary-Liz Shaw
Content Operations Assistant: Shannon Stroud
Editorial Services Administrator: Marie Brannon

Food Editors: James Schend; Peggy Woodward, RD
Recipe Editors: Mary King; Jenni Sharp, RD; Irene Yeh

Test Kitchen & Food Styling Manager:
Sarah Thompson
Test Cooks: Nicholas Iverson (lead),
Matthew Hass, Lauren Knoelke
Food Stylists: Kathryn Conrad (senior),
Leah Rekau, Shannon Roum
Prep Cooks: Megumi Garcia, Melissa Hansen,
Bethany Van Jacobson, Sara Wirtz

Photography Director: Stephanie Marchese
Photographers: Dan Roberts, Jim Wieland
Photographer/Set Stylist: Grace Natoli Sheldon
Set Stylists: Stacey Genaw, Melissa Haberman,
Dee Dee Jacq
Photo Studio Assistant: Ester Robards

Editorial Business Manager: Kristy Martin
Editorial Business Associate: Samantha Lea Stoeger

BUSINESS

Vice President, Group Publisher:
Kirsten Marchioli
Publisher: Donna Lindskog

General Manager, Taste of Home Cooking School:
Erin Puariea
Executive Producer, Taste of Home Online Cooking School: Karen Berner

THE READER'S DIGEST ASSOCIATION, INC.

President and Chief Executive Officer:
Bonnie Kintzer
**Vice President, Chief Operating Officer,
North America:** Howard Halligan
Chief Revenue Officer: Richard Sutton
Chief Marketing Officer: Leslie Dukker Doty
Vice President, Content Marketing & Operation◆
Diane Dragan
**Senior Vice President, Global HR
& Communications:** Phyllis E. Gebhardt, SPHR
Vice President, Brand Marketing: Beth Gorry
Vice President, Chief Technology Officer:
Aneel Tejwaney
Vice President, Consumer Marketing Planning:
Jim Woods

For other Taste of Home books and products,
visit us at tasteofhome.com.

For more Reader's Digest products and informatio◆
visit rd.com (in the United States) or rd.ca (in Cana◆

International Standard Book Number:
978-1-61765-418-3
Library of Congress Control Number: 20159408◆

Cover Photography: Jim Wieland
Set Styling: Dee Dee Jacq
Food Stylist: Sue Draheim

Pictured on front cover:
Hawaiian Beef Sliders, page 86
Pictured on back cover:
Cherry-Brandy Baked Brie, page 9
Feta Bruschetta, page 91
Illustrations on inside cover:
Red_Spruce/Shutterstock.com

Printed in China.
1 3 5 7 9 10 8 6 4 2

LIKE US
facebook.com/tasteofhome

TWEET US
@tasteofhome

FOLLOW US
pinterest.com/taste_of_home

SHOP WITH US
shoptasteofhome.com

SHARE A RECIPE
tasteofhome.com/submit

German Beer Cheese Spread, page 26
Chicken Skewers with Sweet & Spicy Marmalade, page 58

TABLE OF CONTENTS

Ranch Snack Mix,
page 157

Blue Cheese-
Stuffed
Strawberries,
page 113

IMPRESS YOUR GUESTS!

Everyone loves to sample different and delicious foods at parties and gatherings. Appetizers and small plates are the tastiest way to introduce your guests to fun, new flavors. Now you can serve up 201 of the most delectable dips and spreads, juicy chicken wings, dainty tartlets, rolled pinwheels, crunchy munchies and other party starters.

The recipes in this collection come from family cooks like you and have been tested by the experienced home economists in the *Taste of Home* Test Kitchen. So you can rest assured that these tasty tidbits will be a success every time.

You'll also find make-ahead preparation tips, practical pointers for keeping party food hot or cold, helpful hints for serving appetizers, time-saving tips, clear instructions, full-color photos and much more.

So turn to *Taste of Home 201 Appetizers & Small Plates* for an abundance of appealing "A-list" hors d'oeuvres...and make your next party a celebration of flavor!

Guaca
Appetizer Squ
pag

ome your guests to the party with an assortment of fun finger foods
as Bacon & Sun-Dried Tomato Phyllo Tarts on page 66.

rving Up Appetizers

enever you offer friends and family
etizers or snacks, you invite them to
comfortable and share time with you
other guests.

ppetizers can be simple such as dip
h chips for a casual night of TV
ching, heartier fare like sandwiches
pizza for Sunday football, a first
rse in a festive dinner, snacks for a
e group at an open house, or the main
al for a special occasion.

rty Planning

ether simple or fancy, savory or sweet,
or cold, appetizers offer versatility
variety when entertaining. And as an
ed benefit, many appetizers can be
de ahead of time—some even weeks in
ance and then frozen—so you can be

ready for guests at a moment's notice or
relaxed when party time arrives.

When planning which appetizers to
serve, don't overdo it. It's better to
prepare a few good choices than to stress
over making a lot of items. Start with one
spectacular appetizer and then complete
your menu with additional easy but
delicious foods and beverages.

Choose from an assortment of hot, cold
and room temperature foods. Select
recipes that offer a variety of colors,
textures (soft and crunchy) and flavors
(sour, salty, savory, sweet, spicy or subtle).
Mix in one or two lighter options to cater
to guests concerned about calories or fat.
Look for appetizers that make a nice
presentation with no last-minute fussing.

Warm Bacon Cheddar Spread, page

Tips to make your guests comfortable

Simple touches can enhance the comfort of your guests. Here are a few ideas to make your party even more enjoyable:

- Have music in the background to set the mood and still allow conversation to take place at a normal tone.

- Have chairs for people to sit and place them in seating arrangements to encourage conversation.

- If you want your guests to use coasters, have plenty of them available and place them in noticeable locations.

- Have small tables and open surfaces on other furniture, where guests may set down their glasses or plates.

- Have an open floor plan so guests can easily walk from one room to the next. Consider stowing away pieces of furniture that are in the way.

- Place trash containers strategically around the area to prevent clutter from building up.

How Much to Serve

The number of appetizers per person varies according to the leng of the party, the number of guests and the other items on the menu.

FOR A SOCIAL HOUR before dinner, plan on serving three or four different appetizers and allow four to five pieces per person.

FOR AN OPEN-HOUSE AFFAIR, plan serving four to five different appetizers and allow four to six pieces per person per hour.

FOR AN APPETIZER BUFFET that is offered in place of a meal, plan on servi six to eight different appetizers and alle 10 to 14 pieces per person.

FOR LARGER GROUPS, off more types of appetizers. For eight guests, three types may be sufficient, 16 guests about four to five types, and for 25 gues six to eight types. The more variety you serve, the fewer servings of each type you'll need.

Fun-Do Fondue, page 29
Ginger Grapefruit Fizz, page 135

PARTY PLANNING

When serving appetizers, no one wants to run out of food. But the challenge is to know how much will be enough. Here are some guidelines to estimate how much you'll need per person. The greater the variety of appetizers you serve, the fewer of each type you will need.

Appetizers

- ☐ 3 tablespoons dip
- ☐ 2 ounces cheese
- ☐ 3 to 4 cocktail wieners
- ☐ 1 to 2 ounces deli meat
- ☐ 3 tablespoons spread
- ☐ 2 to 4 small egg rolls
- ☐ 3 to 4 meatballs
- ☐ 1 to 2 slices pizza
- ☐ 2 to 4 miniature quiches

Beverages (per hour)

- ☐ In warm weather, you may wish to have additional chilled beverages
- ☐ 1 to 2 cups soda, water or iced tea
- ☐ 6 ounces juice
- ☐ 1 to 2 bottles beer
- ☐ ½ (750ml) bottle wine
- ☐ ¾ cup hot coffee or tea
- ☐ ½ cup punch

Miscellaneous

- ☐ 1 to 2 ounces chips
- ☐ 4 crackers
- ☐ 4 fruit or vegetable dippers
- ☐ ½ ounce mixed nuts
- ☐ 3 to 4 pickle slices or 1 pickle spear
- ☐ 3 to 4 olives
- ☐ 1 to 2 small rolls
- ☐ 3 to 4 ounces ice for beverages

DIPS &
SPREADS

CHERRY-BRANDY BAKED BRIE

Guests will be impressed with this pretty appetizer, but it takes only minutes to create. It is certain to make any occasion special. Substitute dried cranberries or apricots for the cherries, if you like.
—KEVIN PHEBUS KATY, TX

START TO FINISH: 20 MIN.
MAKES: 8 SERVINGS

- **1 round (8 ounces) Brie cheese**
- **½ cup dried cherries**
- **½ cup chopped walnuts**
- **¼ cup packed brown sugar**
- **¼ cup brandy or unsweetened apple juice**
- **French bread baguette, sliced and toasted or assorted crackers**

1. Preheat oven to 350°. Place cheese in a 9-in. pie plate. Combine cherries, walnuts, brown sugar and brandy; spoon over cheese.

2. Bake 15-20 minutes or until cheese is softened. Serve with baguette.

BUFFALO WING CHEESE MOLD

I took a baked version of a hot wing dip and turned it into a cheese ball appetizer. It's great for summertime parties when you don't want to heat up the kitchen.
—DEBORAH HELSER ATTICA, NY

PREP: 40 MIN. + CHILLING
MAKES: 24 SERVINGS

- **2 packages (8 ounces each) cream cheese, softened**
- **2 celery ribs, finely chopped**
- **2 cups (8 ounces) crumbled blue cheese**
- **1 cup (4 ounces) shredded Monterey Jack cheese**
- **1½ cups finely chopped cooked chicken breasts**
- **3 tablespoons buffalo wing sauce**
- **1 French bread baguette (16 ounces)**
- **¼ cup olive oil**
- **½ cup shredded carrots, optional**

1. In a large bowl, combine the cream cheese, celery, blue and Monterey Jack cheeses. In a small bowl, combine chicken and wing sauce.

2. Line a 1-qt. bowl with plastic wrap, overlapping the sides of the bowl. Spread 1½ cups of cream cheese mixture over the bottom and up the sides in prepared bowl. Layer with chicken mixture and remaining cream cheese mixture. Bring plastic wrap over cheese; press down gently. Refrigerate for at least 4 hours or until firm.

3. Just before serving, cut baguette into ¼-in. slices. Place on an ungreased baking sheet; brush with oil. Bake at 375° for 10-12 minutes or until lightly browned.

4. Remove mold from the refrigerator and invert onto a serving plate. Remove bowl and plastic wrap. Garnish with carrots if desired. Serve with toasted baguette slices.

CHUNKY MANGO GUACAMOLE

I recommend you triple or quadruple this chunky guacamole if you're serving a crowd—it's that delicious! To keep prep easy, chop the onion, tomato and mango in advance. Chop the avocado and combine all of the ingredients on the day of the party.
—**DIANA NIENBERG** MCCOMB, OH

START TO FINISH: 15 MIN.
MAKES: 4 CUPS

- 3 medium ripe avocados, peeled and chopped
- 1 large mango, peeled and chopped
- 1 large tomato, chopped
- 1 small red onion, chopped
- ¼ cup chopped fresh cilantro
- 3 tablespoons lime juice
- 1 teaspoon salt
  Assorted fresh vegetables and tortilla chips

In a large bowl, combine the first five ingredients; stir in lime juice and salt. Serve with vegetables and chips.

APPETIZER BLUE CHEESE LOGS

Three kinds of cheese and curry powder make this cheese log a little more lively than most. Guests will like the tasty surprise.
—**ETHEL JOHNSON** NORTH SAANICH, BC

PREP: 20 MIN. + CHILLING
MAKES: 2 CHEESE LOGS

- 1 package (8 ounces) cream cheese softened
- 1 cup (4 ounces) shredded sharp cheddar cheese
- ½ cup crumbled blue cheese
- 1½ teaspoons curry powder
- 1 tablespoon butter
- ½ cup finely chopped pecans
- 2 tablespoons minced fresh parsley
  Assorted crackers

1. In a bowl, beat the cream cheese. Fold in cheddar cheese and blue cheese. Cover and refrigerate for at least 2 hours.

2. In a small skillet, saute curry powder in butter for 1-2 minutes. Stir in pecans; cook and stir for 1 minute. Stir in parsley. Cool slightly. Roll cheese mixture into two logs, about 5 in. long. Roll in pecan mixture. Cover and refrigerate until serving. Serve with crackers.

SHAPING A CHEESE LOG OR CHEESE BALL

Spoon the cheese mixture onto a piece of plastic wrap. Working from the underside of the wrap, roll or pat the mixture into a log or ball. Complete recipe as directed.

Appetizer Blue
Cheese Logs

CREAMY BLACK BEAN SALSA

I love the way sour cream adds richness and tempers the heat in Mexican dishes, so I added it to my favorite salsa. I often double the recipe because it goes so fast.

—DARLENE BRENDEN SALEM, OR

START TO FINISH: 20 MIN.
MAKES: 4 CUPS

- 1 **can (15 ounces) black beans, rinsed and drained**
- 1½ **cups frozen corn, thawed**
- 1 **cup finely chopped sweet red pepper**
- ¾ **cup finely chopped green pepper**
- ½ **cup finely chopped red onion**
- 1 **tablespoon minced fresh parsley**
- ½ **cup sour cream**
- ¼ **cup mayonnaise**
- 2 **tablespoons red wine vinegar**
- 1 **teaspoon ground cumin**
- 1 **teaspoon chili powder**
- ½ **teaspoon salt**
- ¼ **teaspoon garlic powder**
- ⅛ **teaspoon pepper**
  Tortilla chips

In a large bowl, combine the beans, corn, peppers, onion and parsley. Combine the sour cream, mayonnaise, vinegar and seasonings; pour over corn mixture and toss gently to coat. Serve with tortilla chips. Refrigerate leftovers.

CELEBRATION CHEESE BALLS

The ever-popular cheese ball is a simple and impressive addition to any occasion, big or small. Make all three or start with this basic recipe and add your favorite ingredients to create your own customized variations.

—TASTE OF HOME TEST KITCHEN

PREP: 30 MIN. + CHILLING
MAKES: 3 CHEESE BALLS (1 CUP EACH)

- **2 packages (8 ounces each) cream cheese, softened**
- **1 cup grated Parmesan cheese**
- **2 garlic cloves, minced**

PINE NUT-PESTO CHEESE BALL
- **2 tablespoons prepared pesto**
- **2 tablespoons minced fresh basil**
- **2 tablespoons plus ½ cup pine nuts, toasted, divided**

HORSERADISH-BACON CHEESE BALL
- **2 tablespoons prepared horseradish**
- **½ cup crumbled cooked bacon**
- **1 green onion, finely chopped**

SALSA CHEESE BALL
- **2 tablespoons tomato paste**
- **⅛ teaspoon salt**
- **2 tablespoons minced fresh cilantro**
- **1 tablespoon finely chopped onion**
- **1 tablespoon minced seeded jalapeno pepper**
- **Assorted crackers**

In a large bowl, beat the cream cheese, Parmesan cheese and garlic until blended. Divide into three portions.

FOR PINE NUT-PESTO CHEESE BALL *In a small bowl, beat one portion of cream cheese mixture and pesto until blended. Stir in basil. Chop 2 tablespoons pine nuts; stir into cheese mixture. Shape into a ball; roll in remaining pine nuts. Wrap in plastic wrap; chill until firm.*

FOR HORSERADISH-BACON CHEESE BALL *In a small bowl, beat one portion of cream cheese mixture and horseradish until blended. Stir in bacon and onion. Shape into a ball. Wrap in plastic wrap; chill until firm.*

FOR SALSA CHEESE BALL *In a small bowl, beat one portion of cream cheese mixture, tomato paste and salt until blended. Stir in the cilantro, onion and jalapeno. Shape into a ball. Wrap in plastic wrap; chill until firm.*

1. Refrigerate for up to two weeks. Serve with crackers.

NOTE *Wear disposable gloves when cutting hot peppers; the oils can burn skin. Avoid touching your face.*

QUICK BITES

LOADED BAKED POTATO DIP

I never thought of using waffle-cut fries as a scoop for dip until a friend of mine did at a baby shower. They're ideal for my cheesy bacon and chive dip, which tastes just like a baked potato topper.

—ELIZABETH KING DULUTH, MN

START TO FINISH: 10 MIN.
MAKES: 2½ CUPS

- 2 **cups (16 ounces) sour cream**
- 2 **cups (8 ounces) shredded cheddar cheese**
- 8 **center-cut bacon or turkey bacon strips, chopped and cooked**
- ⅓ **cup minced fresh chives**
- 2 **teaspoons Louisiana-style hot sauce**
  Hot cooked waffle-cut fries

In a small bowl, mix the first five ingredients until blended; refrigerate until serving. Serve with waffle fries.

KEEP DIPS COOL

When serving dip on a hot day, it's important to keep it cool. Fill a large glass or plastic serving bowl with ice cubes, crushed ice or ice packs. Fill a smaller bowl with dip and set on top of the ice. Replace the ice as it melts. If you're taking the dip to an outing, put the dip in a small bowl (plastic is best for traveling because it won't break), cover with plastic wrap and put in a cooler. Assemble the ice-filled serving bowl when you get to the picnic.

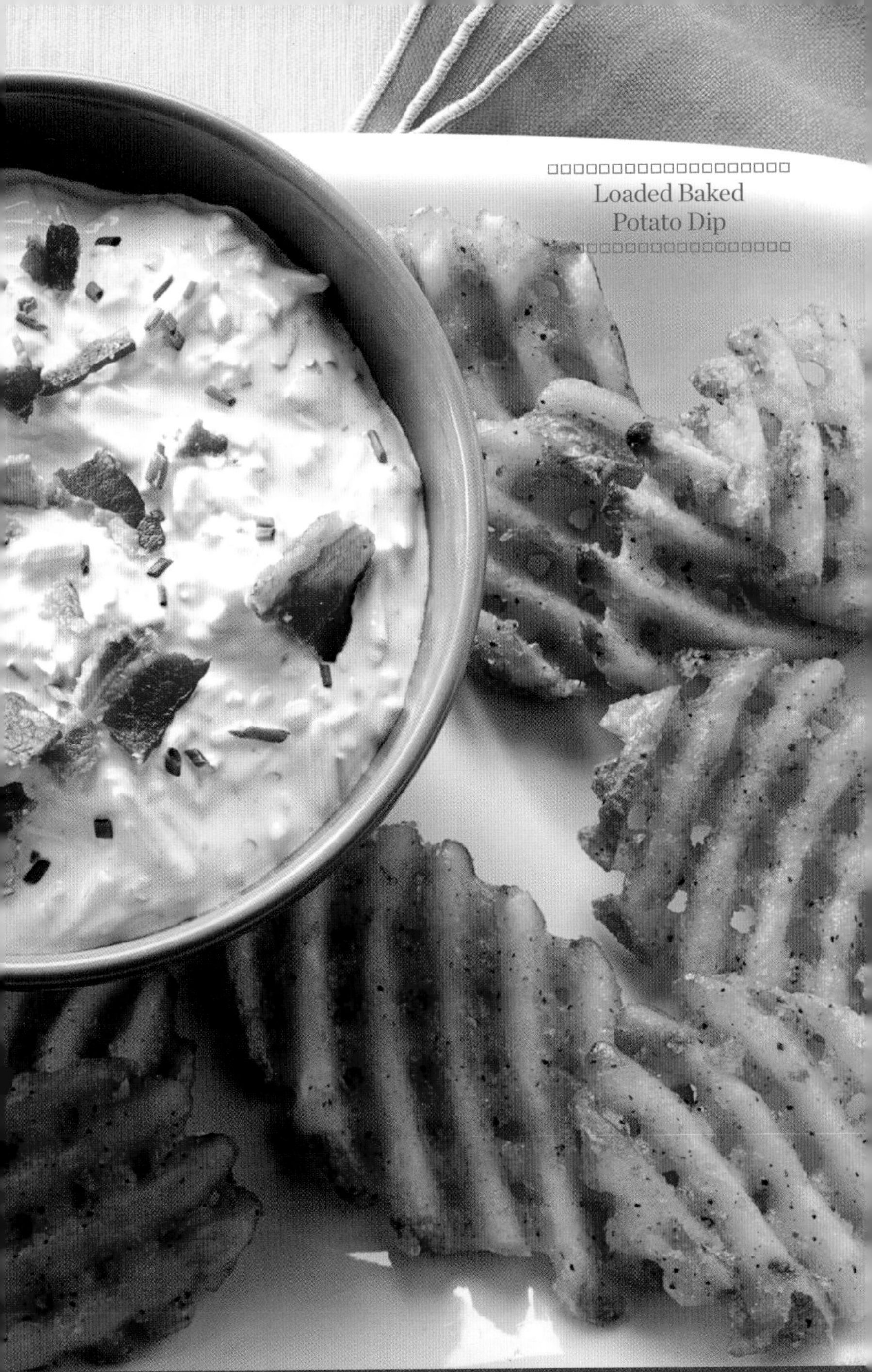

Loaded Baked Potato Dip

SMOKED SALMON CHEESE SPREAD

Pretzels, chips and raw veggies all make delicious dippers for this creamy salmon spread. It's wonderful during the holidays with crackers and wine.

—JILL CAMPBELL HUNTSVILLE, TX

START TO FINISH: 15 MIN.
MAKES: 2½ CUPS

- 2 **packages (8 ounces each) cream cheese, softened**
- 1 **package (4 ounces) smoked salmon or lox**
- 3 **tablespoons horseradish sauce**
- 1 **tablespoon lemon juice**
- 1 **tablespoon Worcestershire sauce**
- ¼ **teaspoon Creole seasoning**
- ¼ **teaspoon coarsely ground pepper**
  Chopped walnuts and snipped fresh dill
  Assorted crackers

Place the first seven ingredients in a food processor; process until blended. Transfer to a serving dish; sprinkle with walnuts and dill. Refrigerate, covered, until serving. Serve with crackers.
NOTE *The following spices may be substituted for 1 teaspoon Creole seasoning: ¼ teaspoon each salt, garlic powder and paprika; and a pinch each of dried thyme, ground cumin and cayenne pepper.*

PEACHY FRUIT DIP

Serve this peachy-keen dip with fresh fruit for a light dessert or side dish. It's even great for breakfast or brunch.
—**BARBARA NOWAKOWSKI**
NORTH TONAWANDA, NY

START TO FINISH: 10 MIN.
MAKES: 1¾ CUPS

- 1 **can (15¼ ounces) sliced or halved peaches, drained**
- ½ **cup marshmallow creme**
- 1 **package (3 ounces) cream cheese, cubed**
- ⅛ **teaspoon ground nutmeg**
  Assorted fresh fruit

In a blender, combine the first four ingredients; cover and blend until smooth. Serve with fruit.

ENLIGHTENED SPICY AVOCADO DIP

Bursting with flavor, this refreshing avocado dip boasts hints of citrus and spice.
—**JESSIE GREARSON-SAPAT**
FALMOUTH, ME

START TO FINISH: 15 MIN.
MAKES: 1½ CUPS

- 2 **medium ripe avocados, peeled and pitted**
- ¼ **cup fresh cilantro leaves**
- ¼ **cup reduced-fat sour cream**
- ¼ **cup lime juice**
- 2 **tablespoons olive oil**
- 1 **garlic cloves, minced**
- ¼ **to ½ teaspoon prepared wasabi**
  Assorted fresh vegetables

Place the first seven ingredients in a food processor; cover and process until smooth. Chill until serving. Serve with vegetables.

HOT COLLARDS AND ARTICHOKE DIP

Spinach and artichoke dip is a perennial favorite at parties and potlucks. Give this classic a southern twist with collard greens in place of spinach. Serve it with warm garlic naan or tortilla chips.
—**BILLIE WILLIAMS-HENDERSON**
BOWIE, MD

PREP: 20 MIN. • **BAKE:** 25 MIN.
MAKES: 24 SERVINGS (¼ CUP EACH)

- 12 **ounces frozen chopped collard greens (about 4 cups), thawed and squeezed dry**
- 2 **jars (7½ ounces each) marinated quartered artichoke hearts, drained and chopped**
- 1 **cup (8 ounces) sour cream**
- 1 **package (6½ ounces) garlic-herb spreadable cheese**
- 1 **cup grated Parmesan cheese**
- 10 **thick-sliced peppered bacon strips, cooked and crumbled**
- ¾ **cup mayonnaise**
- 1½ **cups (6 ounces) shredded part-skim mozzarella cheese, divided**
  Garlic naan flatbreads, warmed and cut into wedges

1. In a large bowl, mix the first seven ingredients and 1 cup mozzarella cheese until blended. Transfer to a greased 11x7-in. baking dish. Sprinkle with remaining mozzarella cheese.
2. Bake, uncovered, at 350° for 20-25 minutes or until heated through and cheese is melted. Serve with naan.

CREAMY ARTICHOKE DIP

PREP: 20 MIN. • **COOK:** 1 HOUR • **MAKES:** 5 CUPS

- 2 cans (14 ounces each) water-packed artichoke hearts, rinsed, drained and coarsely chopped
- 2 cups (8 ounces) shredded part-skim mozzarella cheese
- 1 package (8 ounces) cream cheese, cubed
- 1 cup shredded Parmesan cheese
- ½ cup mayonnaise
- ½ cup shredded Swiss cheese
- 2 tablespoons lemon juice
- 2 tablespoons plain yogurt
- 1 tablespoon seasoned salt
- 1 tablespoon chopped seeded jalapeno pepper
- 1 teaspoon garlic powder
  Tortilla chips

In a 3-qt. slow cooker, combine the first 11 ingredients. Cover and cook on low for 1 hour or until heated through. Serve with tortilla chips.
NOTE *Wear disposable gloves when cutting hot peppers; the oils can burn skin. Avoid touching your face.*

This creamy dip is a family favorite. My sister received this recipe from a friend and passed it along. It's loaded with cheese, artichokes and just the right amount of spice for a crowd-pleasing flavor.
—**MARY SPENCER** GREENDALE, WI

Creamy Artichoke Dip

STRAWBERRY SALSA

Fresh strawberries add sweetness to this fruit salsa while peppers, cilantro and red pepper flakes lend a subtle bite. It's a nice change of pace from typical salsa, and the color makes it a pretty addition to the table.

—NANCY WHITFORD EDWARDS, NY

PREP: 20 MIN. + CHILLING
MAKES: 4 CUPS

- 1½ cups sliced fresh strawberries
- 1½ cups chopped sweet red pepper
- 1 cup chopped green pepper
- 1 cup seeded chopped tomato
- ¼ cup chopped Anaheim pepper
- 2 tablespoons minced fresh cilantro
- ½ teaspoon salt
- ½ teaspoon crushed red pepper flakes
- ¼ teaspoon pepper
- 2 tablespoons plus 2 teaspoons honey
- 2 tablespoons lemon juice

In a large bowl, combine the first nine ingredients. In a small bowl, combine honey and lemon juice; gently stir into the strawberry mixture. Cover and refrigerate for at least 4 hours. Stir just before serving. Serve the salsa with a slotted spoon.

NOTE *Wear disposable gloves when cutting hot peppers; the oils can burn skin. Avoid touching your face.*

BLT DIP

Fans of bacon, lettuce and tomato sandwiches will fall for this dip. It's easy to transport and always draws recipe requests.
—**EMALEE PAYNE** EAU CLAIRE, WI

START TO FINISH: 10 MIN.
MAKES: 6 CUPS

- 2 cups (16 ounces) sour cream
- 2 cups mayonnaise
- 2 pounds sliced bacon, cooked and crumbled
- 6 plum tomatoes, chopped
- 3 green onions, chopped
  Additional crumbled cooked bacon and chopped green onions, optional
  Assorted crackers or chips

In a large bowl, combine the sour cream, mayonnaise, bacon, tomatoes and onions. Refrigerate until serving. Garnish with bacon and onions if desired. Serve with crackers or chips.

MAMMA'S CAPONATA

My Italian mom has been making this versatile appetizer for years. It's great served hot or cold.
—**GEORGETTE STUBIN** CANTON, MI

PREP: 30 MIN. • **COOK:** 40 MIN.
MAKES: 6 CUPS

- 1 large eggplant, peeled and chopped
- ¼ cup plus 2 tablespoons olive oil, divided
- 2 medium onions, chopped
- 2 celery ribs, chopped
- 2 cans (14½ ounces each) diced tomatoes, undrained
- ⅓ cup chopped ripe olives
- ¼ cup red wine vinegar
- 2 tablespoons sugar

- 2 tablespoons capers, drained
- ½ teaspoon salt
- ½ teaspoon pepper
  French bread baguettes, sliced and toasted

1. In a Dutch oven, saute eggplant in ¼ cup oil until tender. Remove from the pan and set aside. In the same pan, saute onions and celery in remaining oil until tender. Stir in tomatoes and eggplant. Bring to a boil. Reduce heat; simmer, uncovered, for 15 minutes.
2. Add the olives, vinegar, sugar, capers, salt and pepper. Return to a boil. Reduce heat; simmer, uncovered, for 20 minutes or until thickened. Serve warm or at room temperature with baguettes.

EGGPLANT 101

When buying eggplant, select those with smooth skin; avoid those with soft or brown spots. Refrigerate for up to 5 days in a plastic bag. Young and tender eggplants do not need to be peeled before using, but larger eggplants may be bitter and will taste better when peeled.

WARM BACON CHEDDAR SPREAD

This is my go-to recipe when I have people over. The warm, luscious dip never disappoints.

—CARA LANGER OVERLAND PARK, KS

PREP: 30 MIN. • **BAKE:** 15 MIN.
MAKES: 3 CUPS

- 1 package (8 ounces) cream cheese, softened
- ½ cup mayonnaise
- ¼ teaspoon dried thyme
- ⅛ teaspoon pepper
- 1 cup (4 ounces) shredded sharp cheddar cheese
- 3 green onions, chopped
- 8 bacon strips, cooked and crumbled, divided
- ½ cup crushed Ritz crackers
  Assorted crackers

1. Preheat oven to 350°. In a large bowl, combine cream cheese, mayonnaise, thyme and pepper. Stir in cheese, green onions and half the bacon. Transfer to a greased 3-cup baking dish.
2. Bake, uncovered, 13-15 minutes or until bubbly. Top with crushed crackers and remaining bacon. Serve with assorted crackers.

BAKED BACON

Instead of frying bacon, lay strips on a jelly roll or foil-lined baking pan and bake at 350° for about 30 minutes. Bacon comes out crisp and flat when prepared this way. Plus, the pan cleans easily, and there's no stove-top spattering to clean up afterwards.

□□□□□□□□□□□□□□□□□□□□□□
**Warm Bacon
Cheddar Spread**
□□□□□□□□□□□□□□□□□□□□□□

CHIPOTLE HAM 'N' CHEESE DIP

PREP: 15 MIN. • **COOK:** 1 HOUR
MAKES: 7 CUPS

- **2 packages (8 ounces each) cream cheese, cubed**
- **1 can (12 ounces) evaporated milk**
- **2 cups (8 ounces) shredded Gouda cheese**
- **1 cup (4 ounces) shredded cheddar cheese**
- **2 tablespoons chopped chipotle pepper in adobo sauce**
- **1 teaspoon ground cumin**
- **2 cups diced fully cooked ham**
  Fresh vegetables or tortilla chips

1. In a 3-qt. slow cooker, combine the first six ingredients. Cover and cook on low for 40 minutes.

2. Stir in ham; cook 20 minutes longer or until heated through. Serve warm with vegetables or chips.

If you like throwing dinner parties for friends, you'll love this convenient slow cooker recipe. Just set the slow cooker on low, put out assorted crackers or vegetables and enjoy visiting with your guests.

—LISA RENSHAW KANSAS CITY, MO

HAM SALAD SPREAD

This hearty ham salad spread has come to be an anticipated leftover every time we have ham for a special dinner. I've passed this recipe on to my daughter and daughter-in-law.

—MARCELLA KULP QUAKERTOWN, PA

START TO FINISH: 15 MIN.
MAKES: 3 CUPS

- 3   cups ground fully cooked ham
- 1   hard-cooked egg, chopped
- 2   tablespoons finely chopped celery
- 2   teaspoons finely chopped onion
- 2   teaspoons sweet pickle relish
- ¾   cup mayonnaise
- 1   tablespoon prepared mustard
      Assorted crackers

In a large bowl, combine the first five ingredients. Combine mayonnaise and mustard; add to ham mixture and mix well. Refrigerate until serving. Serve with crackers.

PEPPERONI PIZZA DIP

This dip is easy to make and transport. You won't have to keep it warm long, because it'll be gone in a flash. It's a great appetizer for any party.

—LISA FRANCIS ELBA, AL

PREP: 20 MIN. • **COOK:** 2½ HOURS
MAKES: 5 CUPS

- 4   cups (16 ounces) shredded
      cheddar cheese
- 4   cups (16 ounces) shredded
      part-skim mozzarella cheese
- 1   cup mayonnaise
- 1   jar (6 ounces) sliced mushrooms,
      drained
- 2   cans (2¼ ounces each) sliced ripe
      olives, drained
- 1   package (3½ ounces) pepperoni
      slices, quartered
- 1   tablespoon dried minced onion
      Assorted crackers

1. In a 3-qt. slow cooker, combine the cheeses, mayonnaise, mushrooms, olives, pepperoni and onion.
2. Cover and cook on low for 1½ hours; stir. Cover and cook 1 hour longer or until heated through. Serve with crackers.

QUICK BITES

GERMAN BEER CHEESE SPREAD

We love the bold flavors of our German heritage. Cheddar and beer make a tangy spread to serve with pretzels, crackers, pumpernickel and sausage. Choose your favorite beer—the flavor comes through in the finished recipe.

—ANGELA SPENGLER TAMPA, FL

START TO FINISH: 15 MIN.
MAKES: 2½ CUPS

- 1 **pound sharp cheddar cheese, cut into ½-inch cubes**
- 1 **tablespoon Worcestershire sauce**
- 1½ **teaspoons prepared mustard**
- 1 **small garlic clove, minced**
- ¼ **teaspoon salt**
- ⅛ **teaspoon pepper**
- ⅔ **cup German beer or nonalcoholic beer**
  Assorted crackers

1. Place cheese in a food processor; pulse until finely chopped, about 1 minute. Add Worcestershire sauce, mustard, garlic, salt and pepper. Gradually add beer, while continuing to process, until mixture is smooth and spreadable, about 1½ minutes.

2. Transfer to a serving bowl or gift jars. Refrigerate, covered, up to 1 week. Serve with crackers.

BAKED REUBEN DIP

I love a good Reuben sandwich, and this recipe combines all of its flavors into a great party dip.

—**SYLVIA METZLER** CHILLICOTHE, OH

PREP: 10 MIN. • **BAKE:** 25 MIN.
MAKES: 8 CUPS

- **1** jar (32 ounces) sauerkraut, rinsed and well drained
- **10** ounces sliced deli corned beef, chopped
- **2** cups (8 ounces) shredded sharp cheddar cheese
- **2** cups (8 ounces) shredded Swiss cheese
- **1** cup mayonnaise
- **¼** cup Russian salad dressing
- **1** teaspoon caraway seeds, optional
  Rye crackers

In a large bowl, mix the first six ingredients; stir in caraway seeds, if desired. Transfer to a greased 13x9-in. baking dish. Bake at 350° for 25-30 minutes or until bubbly. Serve dip with rye crackers.

Fun-Do Fondue

FUN-DO FONDUE

START TO FINISH: 20 MIN. • **MAKES:** 3 CUPS

- 2 **cups (8 ounces) shredded Jarlsberg cheese**
- ½ **cup shredded Swiss cheese**
- ¼ **cup all-purpose flour**
- ½ **teaspoon ground mustard**
- ½ **teaspoon freshly ground pepper**
- 1 **cup heavy whipping cream**
- 1 **cup reduced-sodium chicken broth**
- 1 **tablespoon honey**
- 1 **teaspoon lemon juice**
  Cubed French bread, sliced pears and assorted fresh vegetables

1. In a small bowl, combine the first five ingredients; toss to combine. In a saucepan, combine cream, broth and honey; bring just to a boil, stirring occasionally. Reduce heat to medium-low. Add ½ cup cheese mixture; stir constantly until almost completely melted. Continue adding cheese, ½ cup at a time, allowing cheese to almost melt completely between additions. Continue stirring until thickened and smooth. Stir in lemon juice.

2. Transfer mixture to a heated fondue pot; keep fondue bubbling gently. Serve with bread, pears and vegetables for dipping. If fondue becomes too thick, stir in a little additional broth.

> Fondues are a hit at our gatherings. The younger crowd dips bread cubes, and the adults like apples and pears. Celery, cucumbers and bell peppers work, too.
> —**JUDY BATSON** TAMPA, FL

QUICK BITES

ROASTED RED PEPPER HUMMUS

My son taught me how to make hummus, which is a great alternative to calorie-filled dips. This recipe is simply delicious. Fresh roasted red bell peppers make it special.

—NANCY WATSON-PISTOLE SHAWNEE, KS

PREP: 30 MIN. + STANDING
MAKES: 3 CUPS

- 2 **large sweet red peppers**
- 2 **cans (15 ounces each) garbanzo beans or chickpeas, rinsed and drained**
- ⅓ **cup lemon juice**
- 3 **tablespoons tahini**
- 1 **tablespoon olive oil**
- 2 **garlic cloves, peeled**
- 1¼ **teaspoons salt**
- 1 **teaspoon curry powder**
- ½ **teaspoon ground coriander**
- ½ **teaspoon ground cumin**
- ½ **teaspoon pepper**
  Pita bread, warmed and cut into wedges, and reduced-fat wheat snack crackers
  Additional garbanzo beans or chickpeas, optional

1. Broil red peppers 4 in. from the heat until skins blister, about 5 minutes. With tongs, rotate peppers a quarter turn. Broil and rotate until all sides are blistered and blackened. Immediately place peppers in a bowl; cover and let stand for 15-20 minutes.

2. Peel off and discard charred skin. Remove stems and seeds. Place the peppers in a food processor. Add the beans, lemon juice, tahini, oil, garlic and seasonings; cover and process until blended.

3. Transfer to a serving bowl. Serve with pita bread and crackers. Garnish with additional beans if desired.

TROPICAL DIP

We were inspired by sunny warm climates when we developed this pineapple and coconut fruit dip. Serve it at your next luau or backyard barbecue.

—TASTE OF HOME TEST KITCHEN

PREP: 10 MIN. + CHILLING
MAKES: 2 CUPS

- 1 **can (8 ounces) crushed pineapple, undrained**
- 1 **package (3.4 ounces) instant vanilla pudding mix**
- ¾ **cup cold 2% milk**
- ½ **cup flaked coconut**
- ½ **cup sour cream**
  Toasted coconut
  Assorted fresh fruit

1. In a blender, combine the pineapple, pudding mix, milk, coconut and sour cream; cover and process for 30 seconds.

2. Transfer to a serving bowl; cover and refrigerate for 30 minutes. Garnish with toasted coconut. Serve with fruit.

Tropical Dip

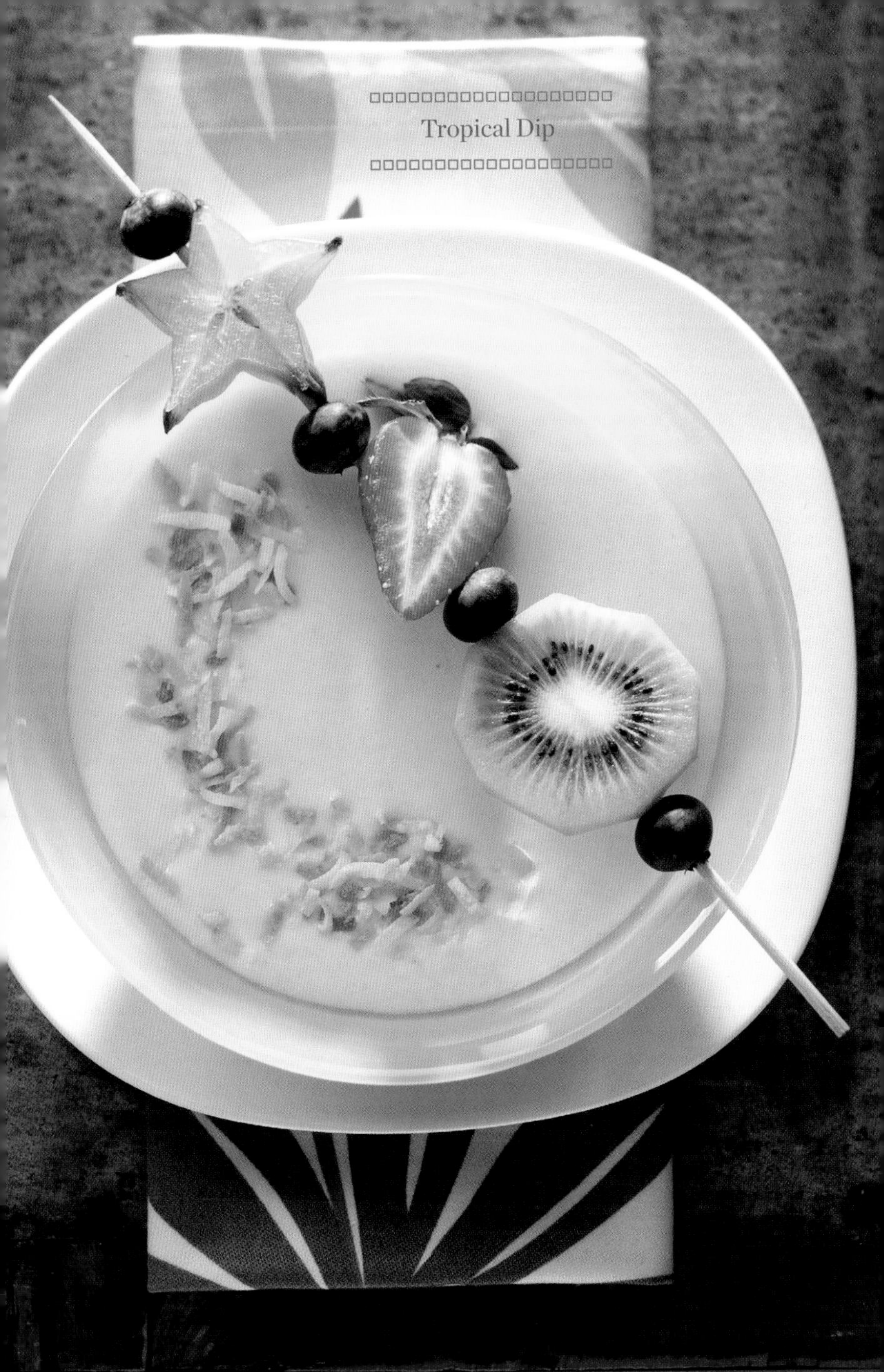

TOMATILLO SALSA

Salsa lovers will appreciate this deliciously fun and addictive tomatillo-based version. It's fantastic as a snack served with tortilla chips or as a condiment to your favorite cut of meat.

—LORI KOSTECKI WAUSAU, WI

START TO FINISH: 20 MIN.
MAKES: 2¼ CUPS

- 8 **tomatillos, husks removed**
- 1 **medium tomato, quartered**
- 1 **small onion, cut into chunks**
- 1 **jalapeno pepper, seeded**
- 3 **tablespoons fresh cilantro leaves**
- 3 **garlic cloves, peeled**
- 1 **tablespoon lime juice**
- ½ **teaspoon salt**
- ¼ **teaspoon ground cumin**
- ⅛ **teaspoon pepper**
  Tortilla chips

1. In a large saucepan, bring 4 cups water to a boil. Add tomatillos. Reduce heat; simmer, uncovered, for 5 minutes. Drain.

2. Place the tomatillos, tomato, onion, jalapeno, cilantro, garlic, lime juice and seasonings in a food processor. Cover and process until blended. Serve with chips.

NOTE *Wear disposable gloves when cutting hot peppers; the oils can burn skin. Avoid touching your face.*

ALMOND "FETA" WITH HERB OIL

Blanched almonds give this appetizer a rich texture. Unbaked, it's smooth and spreadable, while baking makes it crumbly like feta. It's easy to make ahead.

—**MARY RAYMOND** CHESTERFIELD, MO

PREP: 25 MIN. + SOAKING
BAKE: 35 MIN. + CHILLING
MAKES: 1½ CUPS

- 1 **cup blanched almonds**
- ½ **cup water**
- ¼ **cup lemon juice**
- 5 **tablespoons olive oil, divided**
- 1 **garlic clove**
- 1¼ **teaspoons salt**
- 1½ **teaspoons minced fresh thyme or ½ teaspoon dried thyme**
- ½ **teaspoon minced fresh rosemary or ⅛ teaspoon dried rosemary, crushed**
  Assorted crackers

1. Rinse almonds in cold water. Place in a large bowl; add water to cover by 3 in. Cover and let stand overnight.
2. Drain and rinse almonds, discarding liquid. Transfer to a food processor. Add ½ cup water, lemon juice, 3 tablespoons oil, garlic and salt; cover and process for 5-6 minutes or until pureed.
3. Line a large strainer with four layers of cheesecloth and place over a large bowl. Pour almond mixture into prepared strainer; bring up corners of cloth and tie with string to form a bag. Refrigerate overnight.
4. Squeeze out any liquid; remove cheesecloth and discard liquid from bowl. Transfer ball to a parchment paper-lined baking sheet; flatten slightly into a 6-in. circle.
5. Bake at 200° for 35-40 minutes or until firm. Cool. Refrigerate until chilled.
6. In a small skillet, heat the thyme, rosemary and remaining oil over medium heat for 2 minutes. Cool to room temperature. Drizzle over almond mixture. Serve with crackers.

YUMMY CHOCOLATE DIP

START TO FINISH: 10 MIN.
MAKES: 2 CUPS

- ¾ **cup semisweet chocolate chips**
- 1 **carton (8 ounces) whipped topping, divided**
- ½ **teaspoon ground cinnamon**
- ½ **teaspoon rum extract or vanilla extract**
  Assorted fresh fruit or graham cracker sticks

1. In a microwave, melt chocolate chips; stir until smooth. Stir in ½ cup whipped topping, cinnamon and extract; cool for 5 minutes.
2. Fold in remaining whipped topping. Serve with fruit. Refrigerate leftovers.

Turn fresh fruit into an irresistible snack or a dreamy dessert with this creamy chocolate dip. Four ingredients and 10 minutes are all it takes!

—**STACEY SHEW** COLOGNE, MN

PINEAPPLE-PECAN CHEESE SPREAD

This creamy cheese spread is packed with red pepper, green chilies and crunchy pecans. Instead of serving it in a dish, I like to shape it into a ball and roll it in the pecans.
—CYNDE SONNIER MONT BELVIEU, TX

START TO FINISH: 20 MIN.
MAKES: 3¾ CUPS

- 2 **packages (8 ounces each) cream cheese, softened**
- 1½ **cups (6 ounces) shredded cheddar cheese**
- 1 **cup chopped pecans, toasted, divided**
- ¾ **cup crushed pineapple, drained**
- 1 **can (4 ounces) chopped green chilies, drained**
- 2 **tablespoons chopped roasted sweet red pepper**
- ½ **teaspoon garlic powder**
  Assorted fresh vegetables

1. In a large bowl, beat cream cheese until smooth. Add the cheddar cheese, ¾ cup pecans, pineapple, chilies, red pepper and garlic powder; beat until combined. Transfer to a serving dish. Cover and refrigerate until serving.
2. Sprinkle with remaining pecans just before serving. Serve with vegetables.

HOT SAUSAGE & BEAN DIP

I love taking this dip to game-day parties—no one else brings anything like it!
—MANDY RIVERS LEXINGTON, SC

PREP: 25 MIN. • **BAKE:** 20 MIN.
MAKES: 16 SERVINGS (¼ CUP EACH)

- 1 **pound bulk hot Italian sausage**
- 1 **medium onion, finely chopped**
- 4 **garlic cloves, minced**
- ½ **cup dry white wine or chicken broth**
- ½ **teaspoon dried oregano**
- ¼ **teaspoon salt**
- ¼ **teaspoon dried thyme**
- 1 **package (8 ounces) cream cheese, softened**
- 1 **package (6 ounces) fresh baby spinach, coarsely chopped**
- 1 **can (15 ounces) white kidney or cannellini beans, rinsed and drained**
- 1 **cup chopped seeded tomatoes**
- 1 **cup (4 ounces) shredded part-skim mozzarella cheese**
- ½ **cup shredded Parmesan cheese**
  Assorted crackers or toasted French bread baguette slices

1. Preheat oven to 375°. In a large skillet, cook sausage, onion and garlic over medium heat until sausage is no longer pink, breaking up sausage into crumbles; drain. Stir in wine, oregano, salt and thyme. Bring to a boil; cook until liquid is almost evaporated.
2. Add cream cheese; stir until melted. Stir in spinach, beans and tomatoes; cook and stir until spinach is wilted. Transfer to a greased 8-in.-square or 1½-qt. baking dish. Sprinkle with cheeses.
3. Bake 20-25 minutes or until bubbly. Serve with crackers.

AVOCADO SHRIMP SALSA

Salsa gets a southern twist when you add avocado and shrimp. It's delicious scooped up with tortilla chips, spooned over grilled chicken breasts or pork chops, or as a chunky side dish to your favorite entree.

—MARIA RIVIOTTA-SIMMONS

SAN TAN VALLEY, AZ

START TO FINISH: 25 MIN.
MAKES: 6 CUPS

- 1 **pound peeled and deveined cooked shrimp, chopped**
- 2 **medium tomatoes, seeded and chopped**
- 2 **medium ripe avocados, peeled and chopped**
- 1 **cup minced fresh cilantro**
- 1 **medium sweet red pepper, chopped**
- ¾ **cup thinly sliced green onions**
- ½ **cup chopped seeded peeled cucumber**
- 3 **tablespoons lime juice**
- 1 **jalapeno pepper, seeded and chopped**
- 1 **teaspoon salt**
- ¼ **teaspoon pepper**
  Tortilla chips

In a large bowl, combine the first 11 ingredients. Serve with tortilla chips.
NOTE *Wear disposable gloves when cutting hot peppers; the oils can burn skin. Avoid touching your face.*

Creamy Wasabi
Spread

CREAMY WASABI SPREAD

Sesame seeds create an attractive coating for this easy cracker spread. Be sure to watch when you're toasting them as they burn easily. You'll find rice crackers in the ethnic food aisle. You can use any flavor, but the wasabi ones are a personal favorite.

—TAMMIE BALON BOYCE, VA

START TO FINISH: 10 MIN. • **MAKES:** 8 SERVINGS

- 1 **package (8 ounces) cream cheese**
- ¼ **cup prepared wasabi**
- 2 **tablespoons sesame seeds, toasted**
- 2 **tablespoons soy sauce**
  Rice crackers

1. Place cream cheese on a cutting board; split into two layers. Spread wasabi over bottom half; replace top layer.

2. Press both sides into sesame seeds. Place on a shallow serving plate; pour soy sauce around cheese. Serve with crackers.

PICNIC VEGGIE DIP

I served this delicious dip alongside a colorful array of vegetables at a party I hosted years ago. Now it's a popular appetizer with family and friends no matter the occasion.

—SUSAN SCHULLER BRAINERD, MN

PREP: 5 MIN. + CHILLING • **MAKES:** 3 CUPS

- 1 **cup mayonnaise**
- 1 **cup (8 ounces) sour cream**
- 1 **package (1.7 ounces) vegetable soup mix**
- 1 **package (10 ounces) frozen chopped spinach, thawed and squeezed dry**
- 1 **can (8 ounces) water chestnuts, drained and chopped**
  Assorted fresh vegetables

In a large bowl, combine the mayonnaise, sour cream and soup mix. Stir in spinach and water chestnuts. Cover and refrigerate for at least 2 hours. Serve with vegetables.

QUICK BITES

MEDITERRANEAN DIP WITH PITA CHIPS

I love Mediterranean food, so I decided to use those flavors in a dip. My party guests loved it! It's now my potluck staple.

—DENISE JOHANOWICZ MADISON, WI

START TO FINISH: 30 MIN.
MAKES: 3½ CUPS (6 DOZEN CHIPS)

- 12 **pita pocket halves**
  Cooking spray
- 1¾ **teaspoons garlic powder, divided**
- 12 **ounces cream cheese, softened**
- 1 **cup (8 ounces) plain yogurt**
- 1 **teaspoon dried oregano**
- ¾ **teaspoon ground coriander**
- ¼ **teaspoon pepper**
- 1 **large tomato, seeded and chopped**
- 5 **pepperoncini, sliced**
- ½ **cup pitted Greek olives, sliced**
- 1 **medium cucumber, seeded and diced**
- ⅓ **cup crumbled feta cheese**
- 2 **tablespoons minced fresh parsley**

1. Cut each pita half into three wedges; separate each wedge into two pieces. Place on an ungreased baking sheet. Spritz both sides of wedges with cooking spray; sprinkle with 1 teaspoon garlic powder.

2. Bake at 350° for 5-6 minutes on each side or until golden brown. Cool on wire racks.

3. Meanwhile, in a small bowl, beat the cream cheese, yogurt, oregano, coriander, pepper and remaining garlic powder. Spread into a 9-in. pie plate. Top with tomato, pepperoncini, olives, cucumber, feta cheese and parsley. Serve with pita chips.

NOTE *Look for pepperoncinis (pickled peppers) in the pickle and olive section of your grocery store.*

FETA FACTS

Feta is a white, salty, semi-firm cheese. Traditionally it was made from sheep's or goat's milk but is now also made with cow's milk. After feta is formed in a special mold, it's sliced into large pieces, salted and soaked in brine. Although feta cheese is mostly associated with Greek cooking, "feta" comes from the Italian word "fette," meaning slice of food.

Mediterranean Dip
with Pita Chips

SUN-DRIED TOMATO SPREAD

This rich, bubbly spread is sure to please. It's thick yet creamy enough to spread, and the sun-dried tomatoes make it stand out from other dips of its kind.

—VALERIE ELKINTON GARDNER, KS

PREP: 15 MIN. • **BAKE:** 20 MIN.
MAKES: 28 SERVINGS (¼ CUP EACH)

- **2 packages (8 ounces each) cream cheese, softened**
- **2 cups mayonnaise**
- **¼ cup finely chopped onion**
- **4 garlic cloves, minced**
- **1 jar (7 ounces) oil-packed sun-dried tomatoes, drained and chopped**
- **⅔ cup chopped roasted sweet red peppers**
- **2 cups (8 ounces) shredded part-skim mozzarella cheese**
- **2 cups (8 ounces) shredded Italian cheese blend**
- **1 cup shredded Parmesan cheese, divided**
  Assorted crackers

1. In a large bowl, combine the cream cheese, mayonnaise, onion and garlic until blended. Stir in tomatoes and red peppers. Stir in the mozzarella cheese, Italian cheese blend and ¾ cup Parmesan cheese.

2. Transfer to a greased 13x9-in. baking dish. Sprinkle with the remaining Parmesan cheese. Bake, uncovered, at 350° for 18-22 minutes or until edges are bubbly and lightly browned. Serve with crackers.

MARTINI CHEESE DIP

After tasting a delicious cheese dip at a party, I experimented at home and came up with my own version. It's fun to serve in a martini glass alongside colorful fresh vegetables.

—CRYSTAL BRUNS ILIFF, CO

PREP: 10 MIN. + CHILLING
MAKES: 1¼ CUPS

- 1 **package (8 ounces) cream cheese, softened**
- 1 **tablespoon mayonnaise**
- ¼ **cup sliced green olives with pimientos, drained and chopped**
- 2 **to 3 tablespoons vodka**
- 2 **tablespoons olive juice**
- ¼ **teaspoon coarsely ground pepper
  Assorted fresh vegetables**

In a large bowl, beat cream cheese and mayonnaise until blended. Stir in the olives, vodka, olive juice and pepper. Refrigerate for at least 2 hours. Spoon into a martini glass if desired. Serve with vegetables.

JALAPENO POPPER SPREAD

I've been told by fellow party-goers that this recipe tastes exactly like a jalapeno popper. I like that it can be made without much fuss.

—ARIANE MCALPINE PENTICTON, BC

PREP: 10 MIN. • **BAKE:** 25 MIN.
MAKES: 4 CUPS

- **2 packages (8 ounces each) cream cheese, softened**
- **1 cup mayonnaise**
- **½ cup shredded Monterey Jack cheese**
- **¼ cup canned chopped green chilies**
- **¼ cup canned diced jalapeno peppers**
- **1 cup shredded Parmesan cheese**
- **½ cup panko (Japanese) bread crumbs**
  Sweet red and yellow pepper pieces and corn chips

In a large bowl, beat the first five ingredients until blended; spread into an ungreased 9-in. pie plate. Sprinkle with Parmesan cheese; top with bread crumbs. Bake at 400° for 25-30 minutes or until lightly browned. Serve with peppers and chips.

CURRIED CHICKEN CHEESE LOG

The curry is mild in this recipe, so it pleases even people who don't usually like curries.
—**KAREN OWEN** RISING SUN, IN

PREP: 25 MIN. + CHILLING
MAKES: 3 CUPS

- 2 **packages (8 ounces each) cream cheese, softened**
- 1½ **cups finely chopped cooked chicken**
- ⅓ **cup finely chopped celery**
- 2 **tablespoons minced fresh parsley**
- 1 **tablespoon steak sauce**
- ½ **teaspoon curry powder**
- ½ **cup sliced almonds, toasted and coarsely chopped**
  Ritz crackers

In a large bowl, beat cream cheese until smooth. Stir in the chicken, celery, parsley, steak sauce and curry powder. Shape into a 9-in. log. Roll in almonds. Wrap in plastic wrap; refrigerate for at least 2 hours. Serve with crackers.

CLASSIC TEXAS CAVIAR

I adapted this recipe from one in a cookbook, and now I can't imagine a get-together at my house without this quick and healthy appetizer.
—**BECKY OLIVER** FAIRPLAY, CO

PREP: 20 MIN. + CHILLING
MAKES: 5 CUPS

- 2 **cans (15½ ounces each) black-eyed peas, rinsed and drained**
- 1 **can (10 ounces) diced tomatoes and green chilies, drained**
- 1 **medium green pepper, finely chopped**
- 1 **small red onion, finely chopped**

- ½ **cup fat-free Italian salad dressing**
- 2 **tablespoons lime juice**
- ¼ **teaspoon salt**
- ¼ **teaspoon pepper**
- 1 **medium ripe avocado, peeled and cubed**
  Tortilla chips

1. In a large bowl, combine the peas, tomatoes, green pepper and onion. In a small bowl, whisk the dressing, lime juice, salt and pepper. Pour over black-eyed pea mixture and stir to coat. Cover and refrigerate for at least 1 hour.
2. Stir in avocado just before serving. Serve with chips.

HOW TO QUICKLY RIPEN AN AVOCADO

To quickly ripen an avocado, place the avocado in a paper bag with an apple. Poke the bag with a toothpick in several spots and leave at room temperature. The avocado should be ripe in 1 to 3 days.

Sweet Gingered
Chicken Wings

HOT
BITES

SWEET GINGERED CHICKEN WINGS

When I prepare this for a get-together, it's one of the first dishes to disappear. I first tasted the delicious chicken wings years ago when I attended a class on using honey in cooking. I love these so much I also serve them as a main course.

—DEBBIE DOUGAL ROSEVILLE, CA

PREP: 10 MIN. • **BAKE:** 1 HOUR
MAKES: 2 DOZEN

- 1 **cup all-purpose flour**
- 2 **teaspoons salt**
- 2 **teaspoons paprika**
- ¼ **teaspoon pepper**
- 24 **chicken wings (about 5 pounds)**

SAUCE

- ¼ **cup honey**
- ¼ **cup thawed orange juice concentrate**
- ½ **teaspoon ground ginger**
  Minced fresh parsley, optional

1. Preheat oven to 350°. Line two baking sheets with foil; coat with cooking spray.
2. In a large resealable plastic bag, combine flour, salt, paprika and pepper. Add chicken wings, a few at a time; seal bag and toss to coat. Divide wings between prepared baking pans. Bake 30 minutes.
3. In a small bowl, combine honey, orange juice concentrate and ginger; brush over chicken wings. Bake 25-30 minutes or until juices run clear.
4. Preheat broiler. Broil wings 4 in. from heat 1-2 minutes or until lightly browned. If desired, sprinkle with parsley.

CRANBERRY CHILI MEATBALLS

My family and friends look forward to these meatballs at our holiday gatherings. Using packaged meatballs saves precious time in the kitchen. These are just as tasty as homemade—there are never any leftovers!

—AMY SCAMERHORN INDIANAPOLIS, IN

START TO FINISH: 30 MIN.
MAKES: ABOUT 6 DOZEN

- 1 **can (14 ounces) jellied cranberry sauce**
- 1 **bottle (12 ounces) chili sauce**
- ¾ **cup packed brown sugar**
- ½ **teaspoon chili powder**
- ½ **teaspoon ground cumin**
- ¼ **teaspoon cayenne pepper**
- 1 **package (32 ounces) frozen fully cooked homestyle meatballs, thawed**

In a large saucepan over medium heat, combine the first six ingredients; stir until sugar is dissolved. Add meatballs; cook for 20-25 minutes or until heated through, stirring occasionally.

BEEF FONDUE WITH MUSTARD-MAYONNAISE SAUCE

Fondue is fun, but the accompanying sauces are what make these appetizers even more delicious. Creamy, zippy sauce enhances the flavor of the beef.

—RUTH PETERSON JENISON, MI

PREP: 10 MIN. + CHILLING
COOK: 5 MIN./BATCH
MAKES: 6 SERVINGS (ABOUT 1 CUP SAUCE)

- 1 **cup mayonnaise**
- 2 **teaspoons finely chopped onion**
- 2 **teaspoons lemon juice**
- 2 **tablespoons horseradish mustard or spicy brown mustard**
- 1½ **pounds beef tenderloin, cut into ¾-inch cubes**
  Oil for deep-fat frying

1. In a small bowl, combine the mayonnaise, onion, lemon juice and mustard; cover and refrigerate for 30 minutes.

2. Pat meat dry with paper towels. Heat oil in a fondue pot to 375°. Use fondue forks to cook meat in oil until it reaches desired doneness. Serve beef with sauce.

TO MAKE AHEAD *Prepare sauce the day before serving.*

TURKEY-CRANBERRY TARTS

We make these tiny tarts to stand in for the turkey and its trimmings at our casual holiday gatherings.

—NADINE MESCH MOUNT HEALTHY, OH

PREP: 25 MIN. • **BAKE:** 10 MIN.
MAKES: 2½ DOZEN

- ⅓ **cup mayonnaise**
- 4 **teaspoons minced fresh parsley**
- 4 **teaspoons honey mustard**
- ½ **teaspoon chopped seeded jalapeno pepper**
- ⅛ **teaspoon pepper**
- 2 **cups cubed cooked turkey breast**
- ⅓ **cup chopped celery**
- ⅓ **cup dried cranberries, chopped**
- ⅓ **cup shredded Swiss cheese**
- ¼ **cup chopped pecans, toasted**
- 30 **frozen miniature phyllo tart shells**

1. In a large bowl, mix the first five ingredients. Add the turkey, celery, cranberries, cheese and pecans; toss to coat.

2. Arrange tart shells on an ungreased baking sheet. Fill with turkey mixture. Bake at 375° for 10-12 minutes or until heated through. Serve warm.

NOTE *To toast nuts, bake in a shallow pan in a 350° oven for 5-10 minutes or cook in a skillet over low heat until lightly browned, stirring occasionally.*

Turkey-Cranberry
Tarts

PROSCIUTTO-WRAPPED APRICOTS

Dried apricots are stuffed with sweetened Mascarpone cheese and wrapped with prosciutto before baking. The result is an appealing snack for special occasions.

—*TASTE OF HOME* TEST KITCHEN

START TO FINISH: 30 MIN.
MAKES: 2 DOZEN

- ¾ cup **Mascarpone cheese**
- 2 tablespoons **confectioners' sugar**
- ⅛ teaspoon **white pepper**
- 1 package (7 ounces) **dried pitted Mediterranean apricots**
- 12 thin slices **prosciutto**

1. In a small bowl, combine the cheese, confectioners' sugar and pepper. Cut a slit in each apricot; fill with cheese mixture. Cut each slice of prosciutto in half lengthwise; wrap a piece around each apricot and secure with a toothpick.

2. Place in an ungreased 15x10x1-in. baking pan. Bake, uncovered, at 425° for 15-20 minutes or until heated through. Refrigerate leftovers.

BACON-WRAPPED APRICOTS
Substitute 12 slices bacon for the prosciutto. Proceed as directed.

LOBSTER & ARTICHOKE QUESADILLAS

Lobster, artichokes, cheese and spices—my favorite things. Put them together in a quesadilla and it's fantastic fare. I serve these with avocados seasoned with fresh lemon juice and lemon pepper.

—**ALLENE BARY-COOPER** WICHITA FALLS, TX

START TO FINISH: 30 MIN.
MAKES: 6 SERVINGS

- ½ cup grated Parmesan cheese
- ½ cup fat-free mayonnaise
- 1 can (14 ounces) water-packed artichoke hearts, rinsed, drained and chopped
- 4½ teaspoons chopped roasted sweet red pepper
- 1 garlic clove, minced
- 6 flour tortillas (10 inches)
- 1 cup cooked lobster meat or canned flaked lobster meat
- ½ cup shredded part-skim mozzarella cheese

1. In a small bowl, combine the Parmesan cheese, mayonnaise, artichokes, red pepper and garlic. Spread over three tortillas. Top with lobster, mozzarella cheese and remaining tortillas; press down lightly.
2. On a griddle coated with cooking spray, cook quesadillas over medium heat for 2 minutes on each side or until cheese is melted. Cut each quesadilla into six wedges.

CHORIZO DATE RUMAKI

I received this recipe from my sister-in-law who got it from her brother, who is a chef. It is delicious and always disappears quickly.

—**MIRIAM HERSHBERGER**
HOLMESVILLE, OH

PREP: 20 MIN. • **BAKE:** 15 MIN.
MAKES: 32 APPETIZERS

- 1 package (1 pound) sliced bacon
- 4 ounces uncooked chorizo or spicy bulk pork sausage
- 2 ounces cream cheese, cubed
- 32 pitted dates

1. Cut each bacon strip in half. In a large skillet, cook bacon in batches over medium heat until partially cooked but not crisp. Remove to paper towels; drain drippings. Crumble chorizo into the same skillet; cook and stir until fully cooked. Drain. Stir in cream cheese.
2. Carefully cut a slit in the center of each date; fill with cream cheese mixture. Wrap a piece of bacon around each stuffed date; secure with toothpicks. Place on ungreased baking sheets. Bake at 350° for 12-15 minutes or until bacon is crisp.

QUICK BITES

RUSTIC ANTIPASTO TART

Ready-made ingredients make this gorgeous tart a hassle-free appetizer.
—**CHERYL LAMA** ROYAL OAK, MI

PREP: 15 MIN. • **BAKE:** 25 MIN.
MAKES: 12 SERVINGS

- 1 **sheet refrigerated pie pastry**
- 2 **tablespoons prepared pesto**
- 1 **cup shredded part-skim mozzarella cheese, divided**
- 4 **ounces sliced turkey pepperoni**
- 1 **jar (7 ounces) roasted sweet red peppers, drained and thinly sliced**
- 1 **jar (7½ ounces) marinated quartered artichoke hearts, drained**
- 1 **tablespoon water**

1. Unroll pastry onto a parchment paper-lined baking sheet. Spread pesto to within 2 in. of edges; sprinkle with ½ cup cheese. Layer with pepperoni and ¼ cup cheese. Top with red peppers and artichokes; sprinkle with remaining cheese.

2. Fold up edges of pastry over filling, leaving center uncovered. Brush folded pastry with water. Bake at 425° for 25-30 minutes or until crust is golden and cheese is melted. Serve warm.

MIX IT UP

Customize the ingredients on this tart to suit your tastes. Experiment with a variety of add-ons such as pitted Greek or ripe olives, slices of hard salami, prosciutto or deli ham, shredded Monterey Jack or provolone cheese or a sprinkle of basil or oregano.

Rustic Antipasto Tart

Mexican Chicken Meatballs

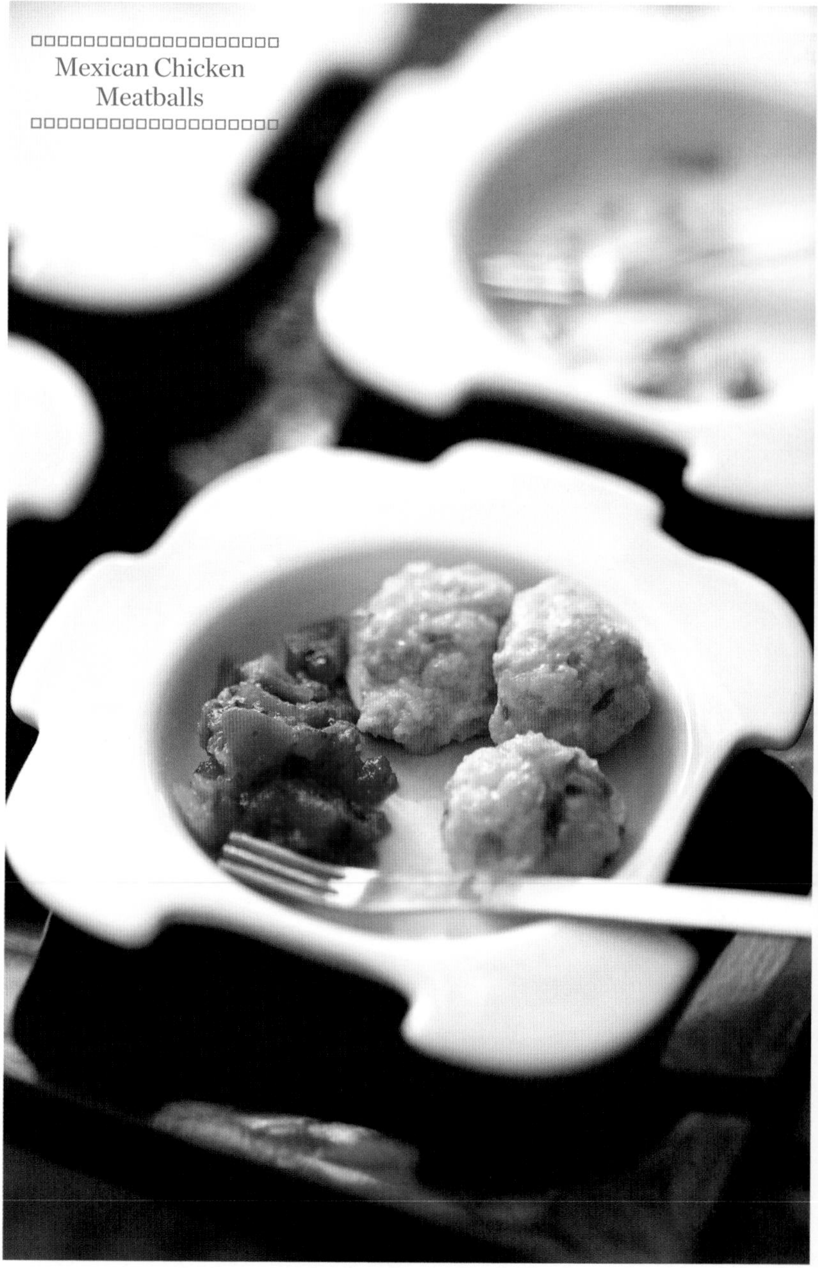

MEXICAN CHICKEN MEATBALLS

PREP: 20 MIN. • **BAKE:** 15 MIN.
MAKES: ABOUT 5 DOZEN

- ½ cup egg substitute
- 1 can (4 ounces) chopped green chilies
- 1 cup crushed cornflakes
- 1 cup (4 ounces) shredded reduced-fat
  Mexican cheese blend
- ½ teaspoon seasoned salt
- ¼ teaspoon cayenne pepper
- 1 pound ground chicken
  Salsa, optional

1. In a large bowl, combine the first six ingredients. Crumble chicken over mixture and mix well. Shape into 1-in. balls. Place on baking sheets coated with cooking spray.

2. Bake at 375° for 12-15 minutes or until a meat thermometer reads 165° and juices run clear, turning occasionally. Serve with salsa if desired.

FREEZE OPTION *Freeze cooled meatballs in freezer containers. To use, partially thaw in refrigerator overnight. Microwave, covered, on high in a microwave-safe dish until heated through, gently stirring and adding a little broth or water if necessary.*

These low-fat meatballs taste fabulous on their own, but if you want to take things up a notch, serve them with a dip of hot Velveeta cheese and salsa. You could also substitute ground white turkey for the chicken.
—**KATRINA LOPES** LYMAN, SC

CARAMELIZED ONION & FIG PIZZA

This is a sensational variation on traditional pizza. It is creamy, sweet and a little salty. The buttery crunch of the pine nuts makes a wonderful accent.

—CONNIE BALBACH BEMIDJI, MN

PREP: 45 MIN. • **BAKE:** 10 MIN.
MAKES: 20 SERVINGS

- 2 **tablespoons olive oil, divided**
- 1 **large onion, chopped**
- 3 **garlic cloves, minced**
- ¼ **teaspoon pepper**
- 1 **tube (13.8 ounces) refrigerated pizza crust**
- 1 **package (8 ounces) cream cheese, softened**
- 1 **teaspoon minced fresh thyme or ¼ teaspoon dried thyme**
- 1 **cup dried figs (about 6 ounces), chopped**
- 6 **thin slices prosciutto or deli ham, chopped**
- ⅓ **cup pine nuts**
- 1 **cup (4 ounces) shredded provolone cheese**

1. In a large skillet, heat 1 tablespoon oil over medium heat. Add onion; cook and stir until softened. Reduce heat to medium-low; cook 30-35 minutes or until deep golden brown, stirring occasionally. Add garlic and pepper; cook 1 minute longer.

2. Preheat oven to 425°. Unroll and press dough onto bottom and up sides of a greased 15x10x1-in. baking pan. Bake 7-10 minutes or until golden brown.

3. In a small bowl, beat cream cheese, thyme and remaining oil until blended. Spread over crust. Top with caramelized onion, figs, prosciutto and pine nuts; sprinkle with cheese. Bake 6-10 minutes longer or until cheese is melted.

TO MAKE AHEAD *This recipe takes minutes to put together when you caramelize the onions the day before.*

APPLE WONTON BUNDLES

These deliciously different treats taste just like caramel apples.

—DARLENE BRENDEN SALEM, OR

PREP: 20 MIN. • **COOK:** 20 MIN.
MAKES: 64 BUNDLES

- 4 **medium tart apples, peeled**
- 64 **wonton wrappers**
- 2 **to 3 cups canola oil**
- 1 **jar (12 ounces) caramel ice cream topping, warmed**

1. Cut each apple into four wedges; cut wedges into four pieces. Place a piece of apple in the center of each wonton wrapper. Brush edges of wrapper with water and bring up around apple; pinch to seal. Cover with plastic wrap until ready to cook.

2. Heat oil in a fondue pot to 375°. Use fondue forks to cook wonton bundles until golden brown (about 1 minute). Cool slightly. Serve bundles with caramel topping.

TERIYAKI STEAK SKEWERS

When these flavorful skewered steaks are sizzling on the grill, the aroma makes everyone around stop what they're doing and come to see what's cooking. The tasty marinade is easy to make, and these little steaks are quick to cook and fun to eat.

—**JERI DOBROWSKI** BEACH, ND

PREP: 15 MIN. + MARINATING
GRILL: 10 MIN. • **MAKES:** 6 SERVINGS

- ½ cup reduced-sodium soy sauce
- ¼ cup cider vinegar
- 2 tablespoons brown sugar
- 2 tablespoons finely chopped onion
- 1 tablespoon canola oil
- 1 garlic clove, minced
- ½ teaspoon ground ginger
- ⅛ teaspoon pepper
- 2 pounds beef top sirloin steak

1. In a large resealable plastic bag, combine the first eight ingredients. Trim fat from steak and slice across the grain into ½-in. strips. Add the beef to bag; seal bag and turn to coat. Refrigerate for 2-3 hours.

2. Drain and discard marinade. Loosely thread meat strips onto six metal or soaked wooden skewers. Grill, uncovered, over medium-hot heat for 7-10 minutes or until meat reaches desired doneness, turning often.

SMOKED MOZZARELLA FLATBREAD PIZZA

Top a refrigerated crust with portobello mushrooms, smoked mozzarella and prosciutto for a hearty starter. Made in a 15x10x1-in. pan, the pizza could even be cut into larger pieces and served as an entree.

—EDWINA GADSBY HAYDEN, ID

PREP: 25 MIN. • **BAKE:** 15 MIN.
MAKES: 24 SERVINGS

- **2 tablespoons butter, divided**
- **2 tablespoons olive oil, divided**
- **⅔ cup sliced red onion**
- **½ pound sliced baby portobello mushrooms**
- **1 garlic clove, minced**
- **2 teaspoons minced fresh rosemary or ½ teaspoon dried rosemary, crushed**
- **1 tube (13.8 ounces) refrigerated pizza crust**
- **1½ cups (6 ounces) shredded smoked mozzarella cheese**
- **2 ounces sliced prosciutto or deli ham, finely chopped**

1. Preheat oven to 400°. In a large skillet, heat 1 tablespoon butter and 1 tablespoon oil over medium-high heat. Add onion; cook and stir 2-3 minutes or until softened. Reduce heat to medium-low; cook 8-10 minutes or until golden brown, stirring occasionally. Remove from pan.

2. In same skillet, heat remaining butter and oil over medium-high heat. Add mushrooms; cook and stir 2-3 minutes or until tender. Add garlic and rosemary; cook about 1-2 minutes longer or until liquid is evaporated.

3. Unroll and press dough onto bottom of a greased 15x10x1-in. baking pan. Using fingertips, press several dimples into dough. Sprinkle with ½ cup cheese; top with onion, mushroom mixture and prosciutto. Sprinkle with remaining cheese. Bake pizza 15-18 minutes or until golden brown and the cheese is melted.

MEDITERRANEAN NACHOS

PREP: 30 MIN.+ STANDING
COOK: 15 MIN. • **MAKES:** 12 SERVINGS

- 2 **medium cucumbers, peeled, seeded and grated**
- 1½ **teaspoons salt, divided**
- ½ **teaspoon ground cumin**
- ½ **teaspoon ground coriander**
- ½ **teaspoon paprika**
- ¾ **teaspoon pepper, divided**
- 6 **whole pita breads**
  Cooking spray
- 1 **pound ground lamb or beef**
- 2 **garlic cloves, minced**
- 1 **teaspoon cornstarch**
- ½ **cup beef broth**
- 2 **cups plain Greek yogurt**
- 2 **tablespoons lemon juice**
- ¼ **teaspoon grated lemon peel**
- 2 **cups torn romaine**
- 2 **medium tomatoes, seeded and chopped**
- ½ **cup pitted Greek olives, sliced**
- 4 **green onions, thinly sliced**
- ½ **cup crumbled feta cheese**

1. In a colander set over a bowl, toss cucumbers with ½ teaspoon salt. Let stand 30 minutes. Squeeze and pat dry. Set aside. In a small bowl, combine the cumin, coriander, paprika, ½ teaspoon pepper and ½ teaspoon salt; set aside.

2. Cut each pita into eight wedges; arrange in a singer layer on ungreased baking sheets. Spritz both sides of pitas with cooking spray; sprinkle with ¾ teaspoon seasoning mix. Broil 3-4 in. from the heat for 3-4 minutes on each side or until golden brown. Cool on wire racks.

3. In a large skillet, cook lamb and remaining seasoning mix over medium heat until lamb is no longer pink. Add garlic; cook 1 minute longer. Drain. Combine cornstarch and broth until smooth; gradually stir into the pan. Bring to a boil; cook and stir for 2 minutes or until thickened.

4. In a small bowl, combine the yogurt, lemon juice, lemon peel, cucumbers and remaining salt and pepper. Arrange pita wedges on a serving platter. Layer with lettuce, lamb mixture, tomatoes, olives, onions and cheese. Serve immediately with cucumber sauce.

NOTE *If Greek yogurt is not available in your area, line a strainer with a coffee filter and place over a bowl. Place 4 cups plain yogurt in prepared strainer; refrigerate overnight. Discard liquid from bowl; proceed as directed.*

> Make a Mediterranean version of nachos using crisped pita wedges topped with ground lamb or beef, feta cheese and a creamy cucumber sauce.
> —**ZAZA FULLMAN-KASL** VENTURA, CA

_____
_____
_____
_____
_____
_____
_____
_____
_____
_____
_____
_____
_____
_____
_____
_____
_____
_____
_____
_____
_____
_____
_____
_____
_____
_____
_____
_____
_____
_____
_____
_____
_____
_____
_____
_____
_____

CHICKEN SKEWERS WITH SWEET & SPICY MARMALADE

My father-in-law loved this chicken dish and said that it reminded him of food he had growing up. We love that it's a tasty meat you can enjoy on a stick.

—LAUREL DALZELL MANTECA, CA

PREP: 25 MIN. + MARINATING • **BROIL:** 5 MIN.
MAKES: 8 SERVINGS (1 CUP SAUCE)

- 1 **pound boneless skinless chicken breasts**
- ¼ **cup olive oil**
- ¼ **cup reduced-sodium soy sauce**
- 2 **garlic cloves, minced**
- ⅛ **teaspoon pepper**

SAUCE
- 2 **teaspoons butter**
- 2 **tablespoons chopped seeded jalapeno pepper**
- 1 **teaspoon minced fresh gingerroot**
- ¾ **cup orange marmalade**
- 1 **tablespoon lime juice**
- 1 **tablespoon thawed orange juice concentrate**
- ¼ **teaspoon salt**

1. Preheat broiler. Pound chicken breasts with a meat mallet to ¼-in. thickness; cut lengthwise into 1-in.-wide strips. In a large resealable plastic bag, combine oil, soy sauce, garlic and pepper. Add chicken; seal bag and turn to coat. Refrigerate 4 hours or overnight.

2. In a small saucepan, heat butter over medium-high heat. Add jalapeno; cook and stir until tender. Add ginger; cook 1 minute longer. Reduce heat; stir in marmalade, lime juice, orange juice concentrate and salt.

3. Drain chicken, discarding marinade. Thread chicken strips, weaving back and forth, onto eight metal or soaked wooden skewers. Place in a greased 15x10x1-in. baking pan. Broil 6 in. from heat 2-4 minutes on each side or until chicken is no longer pink. Serve with sauce.

NOTE *Wear disposable gloves when cutting hot peppers; the oils can burn skin. Avoid touching your face.*

Chicken Skewers with
Sweet & Spicy Marmalade

GRILLED STEAK APPETIZERS WITH STILTON SAUCE

Here's a hearty appetizer that will get any gathering off to a delicious start. The rich, creamy cheese sauce complements the grilled steak to perfection.

—RADELLE KNAPPENBERGER OVIEDO, FL

PREP: 25 MIN. • **GRILL:** 10 MIN.
MAKES: 20 APPETIZERS (¾ CUP SAUCE)

- **2 boneless beef top loin steaks (8 ounces each)**
- **¼ teaspoon salt**
- **¼ teaspoon pepper**
- **½ cup white wine or chicken broth**
- **⅓ cup heavy whipping cream**
- **3 tablespoons sour cream**
- **2 ounces Stilton cheese, cubed**

1. Sprinkle steaks with salt and pepper. Grill steaks, covered, over medium heat for 4-6 minutes on each side or until meat reaches desired doneness (for medium-rare, a meat thermometer should read 145°; medium, 160°; well-done, 170°). Remove meat to a cutting board and keep warm.

2. In a small saucepan, bring wine to a boil; cook until reduced by half. Add cream. Bring to a gentle boil. Reduce heat; simmer, uncovered, until thickened, stirring occasionally. Remove from the heat. Add sour cream and cheese; stir until cheese is melted.

3. Cut steaks into 1-in. cubes; skewer with toothpicks. Serve with sauce.

NOTE *Top loin steak may be labeled as strip steak, KS City steak, NY strip steak, ambassador steak or boneless club steak in your region. You may substitute 1/3 cup crumbled blue cheese for the Stilton cheese.*

ASIAN CHICKEN DUMPLINGS

I enjoy making Chinese food to celebrate my daughters' heritage, especially around holidays such as Chinese New Year. I modified a traditional pork dumpling recipe to use ground chicken.

—JOY OLCOTT MILLERSVILLE, PA

PREP: 40 MIN. • **COOK:** 10 MIN./BATCH
MAKES: 2½ DOZEN

- 1 **pound ground chicken**
- 4 **green onions, chopped**
- ½ **cup chopped cabbage**
- ¼ **cup minced fresh cilantro**
- 2 **teaspoons minced fresh gingerroot**
- 1 **teaspoon salt**
- ¼ **teaspoon Chinese five-spice powder**
- 2 **tablespoons water**
- 1 **package (10 ounces) pot sticker or gyoza wrappers**
  Cabbage leaves
  Reduced-sodium soy sauce

1. Place the first seven ingredients in a food processor; cover and process until finely chopped. Add water; cover and process until blended.

2. Place 1 tablespoon chicken mixture in the center of one wrapper. (Keep remaining wrappers covered with a damp paper towel to prevent them from drying out.) Moisten edges with water. Fold wrapper over filling to form a semicircle; press edges firmly to seal, pleating the front side to form three to five folds.

3. Holding sealed edges, stand each dumpling on an even surface; press to flatten bottom. Repeat with remaining wrappers and filling; cover dumplings with plastic wrap.

4. Line a steamer basket with four cabbage leaves. Arrange dumplings in batches 1 in. apart over cabbage; place in a large saucepan over 1 in. of water. Bring to a boil; cover and steam for 10-12 minutes or until a thermometer reads 165°. Discard cabbage. Repeat. Serve with soy sauce.

QUICK BITES

PEAR-BLUE CHEESE TARTLETS

Blue cheese, pears and walnuts combine in these sensational bite-sized morsels. They're easy to make but look impressive.

—HEIDI DER STOW, OH

PREP: 25 MIN. • **BAKE:** 10 MIN.
MAKES: 2½ DOZEN

- 2 tablespoons butter
- 2 large pears, peeled and finely chopped
- 2 tablespoons honey
  Dash salt
- ¼ cup mascarpone cheese
- ¼ cup crumbled blue cheese
- 2 packages (1.9 ounces each) frozen miniature phyllo tart shells
- ¼ cup finely chopped walnuts

1. Preheat oven to 350°. In a skillet, heat butter over medium-high heat. Add pears; cook and stir 2-3 minutes or until tender. Stir in honey and salt; cook 4-5 minutes longer or until pears are lightly browned. Remove from heat; cool slightly. Stir in cheeses.
2. Place tart shells on an ungreased baking sheet. Fill each with 1½ teaspoons filling; sprinkle with walnuts. Bake tarts 6-8 minutes or until golden brown. Serve tarts warm. Refrigerate any leftovers.

SPICY BEEF SKEWERS

The fragrant spices and full flavors of North Africa make these meaty appetizers popular party food.

—ROXANNE CHAN ALBANY, CA

PREP: 35 MIN. • **BROIL:** 5 MIN.
MAKES: 2 DOZEN (½ CUP SAUCE)

- 1 cup white wine vinegar
- ¾ cup sugar
- ½ cup water
- 1 tablespoon orange marmalade
- ¼ teaspoon grated orange peel
- ¼ teaspoon crushed red pepper flakes
- ½ cup finely chopped salted roasted almonds
- 2 tablespoons minced fresh mint
- 1 green onion, finely chopped
- 1 tablespoon lemon juice
- 1 garlic clove, minced
- ¼ teaspoon each ground cinnamon, cumin and coriander
- 1 pound lean ground beef (90% lean)
  Minced fresh parsley

1. In a small saucepan, combine the first six ingredients. Bring to a boil. Reduce heat; simmer, uncovered, about 25 minutes or until reduced to ½ cup.
2. Meanwhile, in a large bowl, combine almonds, mint, onion, lemon juice, garlic and spices. Crumble beef over mixture and mix well. Divide into 24 pieces. Shape each piece into a 3x1-in. rectangle; insert a soaked wooden appetizer skewer into each.
3. Broil 6 in. from the heat 2-4 minutes on each side or until a thermometer reads 160°. Arrange on a serving platter. Drizzle with sauce mixture and sprinkle with parsley.

ITALIAN MEATBALL BUNS

One of the greatest gifts I love to share with my six grandkids is making special recipes just for them. The meatballs inside these rolls are a savory surprise.

—TRINA LINDER-MOBLEY CLOVER, SC

PREP: 30 MIN. + RISING • **BAKE:** 15 MIN.
MAKES: 2 DOZEN

- **12 frozen bread dough dinner rolls**
- **1 package (12 ounces) frozen fully cooked Italian meatballs, thawed**
- **2 tablespoons olive oil**
- **¼ cup grated Parmesan cheese**
- **¼ cup minced fresh basil**
- **1½ cups marinara sauce, warmed**

1. Let bread dough stand at room temperature 25-30 minutes or until softened.

2. Cut each roll in half. Wrap each portion around a meatball, enclosing meatball completely; pinch dough firmly to seal. Place on greased baking sheets, seam side down. Cover with kitchen towels; let rise in a warm place until almost doubled, about 1½ to 2 hours.

3. Preheat oven to 350°. Bake buns 12-15 minutes or until golden brown. Brush tops with oil; sprinkle with cheese and basil. Serve with warm marinara sauce.

Grilled Cheese &
Tomato Flat Breads

GRILLED CHEESE & TOMATO FLATBREADS

This is a combination of grilled pizza and a cheesy flatbread recipe I discovered years ago. It's a great appetizer or main dish.

—TINA REPAK MIRILOVICH JOHNSTOWN, PA

PREP: 30 MIN. • **GRILL:** 5 MIN.
MAKES: 2 FLATBREADS (12 SERVINGS EACH)

- 1 **package (8 ounces) cream cheese, softened**
- ⅔ **cup grated Parmesan cheese, divided**
- 2 **tablespoons minced fresh parsley, divided**
- 1 **tablespoon minced chives**
- 2 **garlic cloves, minced**
- ½ **teaspoon minced fresh thyme**
- ¼ **teaspoon salt**
- ¼ **teaspoon pepper**
- 1 **tube (13.8 ounces) refrigerated pizza crust**
- 2 **tablespoons olive oil**
- 3 **medium tomatoes, thinly sliced**

1. In a small bowl, beat the cream cheese, ⅓ cup Parmesan cheese, 1 tablespoon parsley, chives, garlic, thyme, salt and pepper until blended.

2. Unroll pizza crust and cut in half. On a lightly floured surface, roll out each portion into a 12x6-in. rectangle; brush each side with oil. Grill, covered, over medium heat for 1-2 minutes or until bottoms are lightly browned. Remove from the grill.

3. Spread grilled sides with cheese mixture. Sprinkle with remaining Parmesan cheese; top with tomatoes. Return to the grill. Cover and cook for 2-3 minutes or until crust is lightly browned and cheese is melted, rotating halfway through cooking to ensure an evenly browned crust. Sprinkle with remaining parsley.

BACON & SUN-DRIED TOMATO PHYLLO TARTS

Frozen mini phyllo tart shells are easy to use and convenient. Just add a savory filling with sun-dried tomatoes and bacon, then pop them in the oven.

—PATRICIA QUINN OMAHA, NE

PREP: 40 MIN. • **BAKE:** 10 MIN.
MAKES: 45 TARTLETS

- 2 teaspoons olive oil
- ¾ cup chopped onion (about 1 medium)
- ¾ cup chopped green pepper (about 1 small)
- ¾ cup chopped sweet red pepper (about 1 small)
- 1 garlic clove, minced
  Dash dried oregano
- 3 packages (1.9 ounces each) frozen miniature phyllo tart shells
- 1 package (8 ounces) cream cheese, softened
- 1½ teaspoons lemon juice
- ⅛ teaspoon salt
- 1 egg, lightly beaten
- ½ cup oil-packed sun-dried tomatoes, chopped and patted dry
- 2 bacon strips, cooked and crumbled
- 1 tablespoon minced fresh basil or 1 teaspoon dried basil
- ½ cup crushed butter-flavored crackers
- ½ cup shredded cheddar cheese

1. Preheat oven to 350°. In a large skillet, heat oil over medium-high heat. Add onion and peppers; cook and stir 6-8 minutes or until tender. Add garlic and oregano; cook 1 minute longer. Cool completely.

2. Place tart shells on ungreased baking sheets. In a large bowl, beat cream cheese, lemon juice and salt until smooth. Add egg; beat on low speed just until blended. Stir in tomatoes, bacon, basil and onion mixture.

3. Spoon 2 teaspoons filling into each tart shell. Top each with ½ teaspoon crushed crackers and ½ teaspoon cheddar cheese.

4. Bake 10-12 minutes or until set. Serve warm.

FREEZE OPTION *Freeze cooled baked pastries in freezer containers. To use, reheat pastries on a baking sheet in a preheated 350° oven 15-18 minutes or until heated through.*

HOMEMADE PHYLLO TART SHELLS

Don't have frozen mini phyllo tart shells on hand? Make your own! Layer three 4½-inch squares of phyllo dough spritzed with water on alternating angles so the corners do not overlap. Gently press into muffin cup. Sprinkle with sugar and spritz with butter-flavored cooking spray. Bake, cool and fill according to recipe.

CRAWFISH BEIGNETS WITH CAJUN DIPPING SAUCE

Get a taste of the deep South with these slightly spicy beignets. You won't be able to eat just one!

—**DONNA LANCLOS** LAFAYETTE, LA

PREP: 20 MIN. • **COOK:** 5 MIN./BATCH
MAKES: ABOUT 2 DOZEN (¾ CUP SAUCE)

- 1   **egg, beaten**
- 1   **pound chopped cooked crawfish tail meat or shrimp**
- 4   **green onions, chopped**
- 1½ **teaspoons butter, melted**
- ½   **teaspoon salt**
- ½   **teaspoon cayenne pepper**
- ⅓   **cup bread flour**
     Oil for deep-fat frying
- ¾   **cup mayonnaise**
- ½   **cup ketchup**
- ¼   **teaspoon prepared horseradish, optional**
- ¼   **teaspoon hot pepper sauce**

1. In a large bowl, combine the egg, crawfish, onions, butter, salt and cayenne. Stir in flour until blended.

2. In an electric skillet or deep fryer, heat oil to 375°. Drop tablespoonfuls of batter, a few at a time, into hot oil. Fry until golden brown on both sides. Drain on paper towels.

3. In a small bowl, combine the mayonnaise, ketchup, horseradish if desired and pepper sauce. Serve with beignets.

SPANAKOPITA PINWHEELS

I'm a fan of spanakopita, a traditional Greek spinach pie, and this recipe is a fun and easy take on it. I've taken these to get-togethers with fellow teachers and colleagues as well as potlucks and family gatherings. They're great with a glass of white wine.

—RYAN PALMER WINDHAM, ME

PREP: 30 MIN. + COOLING • **BAKE:** 20 MIN.
MAKES: 2 DOZEN

- 1 **medium onion, finely chopped**
- 2 **tablespoons olive oil**
- 1 **teaspoon dried oregano**
- 1 **garlic clove, minced**
- 2 **packages (10 ounces each) frozen chopped spinach, thawed and squeezed dry**
- 2 **cups (8 ounces) crumbled feta cheese**
- 2 **eggs, lightly beaten**
- 1 **package (17.3 ounces) frozen puff pastry, thawed**

1. In a small skillet, saute onion in oil until tender. Add oregano and garlic; cook 1 minute longer. Add spinach; cook 3 minutes longer or until liquid is evaporated. Transfer spinach mixture to a large bowl; cool.

2. Add feta cheese and eggs to spinach mixture; mix well. Unfold puff pastry. Spread each sheet with half the spinach mixture to within 1/2 in. of edges. Roll up jelly-roll style. Cut each into twelve 3/4-in. slices. Place cut side down on greased baking sheets.

3. Bake at 400° for 18-22 minutes or until golden brown. Serve warm.

MIXED OLIVE CROSTINI

START TO FINISH: 25 MIN.
MAKES: 2 DOZEN

- 1 **can (4¼ ounces) chopped ripe olives**
- ½ **cup pimiento-stuffed olives, finely chopped**
- ½ **cup grated Parmesan cheese**
- ¼ **cup butter, softened**
- 1 **tablespoon olive oil**
- 2 **garlic cloves, minced**
- ¾ **cup shredded part-skim mozzarella cheese**
- ¼ **cup minced fresh parsley**
- 1 **French bread baguette (10½ ounces)**

1. In a small bowl, combine the first six ingredients; stir in mozzarella cheese and parsley. Cut baguette into 24 slices; place on an ungreased baking sheet. Spread with olive mixture.
2. Broil 3-4 in. from the heat for 2-3 minutes or until edges are lightly browned and cheese is melted.

> These little toasts are irresistible and always a hit. They're a cinch to make and call for ingredients you likely have stocked in the pantry.
> **—LAURIE LACLAIR**
> NORTH RICHLAND HILLS, TX

CHAMPION CHICKEN PUFFS

My guests peeled rubber getting to the table to munch on these tender little bites that are made with hassle-free refrigerated crescent rolls and a flavorful chicken and cream-cheese filling.
—AMBER KIMMICH POWHATAN, VA

START TO FINISH: 30 MIN.
MAKES: 32 APPETIZERS

- 4 **ounces cream cheese, softened**
- ½ **teaspoon garlic powder**
- ½ **cup shredded cooked chicken**
- 2 **tubes (8 ounces each) refrigerated crescent rolls**

1. In a small bowl, beat cream cheese and garlic powder until smooth. Stir in chicken.
2. Unroll crescent dough; separate into 16 triangles. Cut each triangle in half lengthwise, forming two triangles. Place 1 teaspoon of chicken mixture in the center of each. Fold short side over filling; press sides to seal and roll up.
3. Place 1 in. apart on greased baking sheets. Bake at 375° for 12-14 minutes or until golden brown. Serve warm.

MINIATURE SHEPHERD'S PIES

Miniature pies, sweet or savory, are ideal party nibbles. I knew shepherd's pie, a perennial favorite, would be perfect scaled down. I've also made the pies with ground lamb and a teaspoon of dried rosemary.
—**SUZANNE BANFIELD** BASKING RIDGE, NJ

PREP: 40 MIN. • **BAKE:** 15 MIN.
MAKES: 4 DOZEN

- ½ **pound ground beef**
- ⅓ **cup finely chopped onion**
- ¼ **cup finely chopped celery**
- 3 **tablespoons finely chopped carrot**
- 1½ **teaspoons all-purpose flour**
- 1 **teaspoon dried thyme**
- ¼ **teaspoon salt**
- ⅛ **teaspoon ground nutmeg**
- ⅛ **teaspoon pepper**
- ⅔ **cup beef broth**
- ⅓ **cup frozen petite peas**
- 2 **packages (17.3 ounces each) frozen puff pastry, thawed**
- 3 **cups mashed potatoes**

1. Preheat oven to 400°. In a large skillet, cook beef, onion, celery and carrot over medium heat until beef is no longer pink; drain. Stir in flour, thyme, salt, nutmeg and pepper until blended; gradually add broth. Bring to a boil; cook and stir 2 minutes or until sauce is thickened. Stir in peas; heat through. Set aside.

2. Unfold puff pastry. Using a floured 2¼-in. round cutter, cut 12 circles from each sheet (save scraps for another use). Press puff pastry circles onto the bottoms and up the sides of ungreased miniature muffin cups.

3. Fill each with 1½ teaspoons beef mixture; top or pipe with 1 tablespoon mashed potatoes. Bake 13-16 minutes or until heated through and potatoes are lightly browned. Serve warm.

BRIE-APPLE PASTRY BITES

Pop one of these tasty morsels into your mouth for a tangy burst of flavor. For variety, make half with just apples and walnuts and the remainder with cranberries and walnuts.
—**JUDIE THURSTENSON** COLCORD, OK

PREP: 30 MIN. • **BAKE:** 15 MIN.
MAKES: 4 DOZEN

- 1 **package (17.3 ounces) frozen puff pastry, thawed**
- 1 **round (8 ounces) Brie cheese, cut into ½-inch cubes**
- 1 **medium apple, chopped**
- ⅔ **cup sliced almonds**
- ½ **cup chopped walnuts**
- ¼ **cup dried cranberries**
  Ground nutmeg

1. Unfold puff pastry; cut each sheet into 24 squares. Gently press squares onto the bottoms of 48 greased miniature muffin cups.

2. Combine the cheese, apple, nuts and cranberries; spoon into cups. Bake at 375° for 12-15 minutes or until cheese is melted. Sprinkle with nutmeg.

SWEDISH MEATBALLS

I'm a "Svenska flicka" (Swedish girl) from northwest Iowa, where many Swedes settled at the turn of the century. This recipe was given to me by a Swedish friend. It's a 20th century version of a 19th century favorite, since back then they didn't have bouillon cubes or evaporated milk. I think you'll agree that these modern-day "Kottbullar" are very tasty.

—EMILY GOULD HAWARDEN, IA

PREP: 15 MIN. • **COOK:** 20 MIN.
MAKES: 3½ DOZEN

- ⅔ **cup evaporated milk**
- ⅔ **cup chopped onion**
- ¼ **cup fine dry bread crumbs**
- ½ **teaspoon salt**
- ½ **teaspoon allspice**
  Dash pepper
- 1 **pound lean ground beef (90% lean)**
- 2 **teaspoons butter**
- 2 **teaspoons beef bouillon granules**
- 1 **cup boiling water**
- ½ **cup cold water**
- 2 **tablespoons all-purpose flour**
- 1 **cup evaporated milk**
- 1 **tablespoon lemon juice**

1. Combine ⅔ cup evaporated milk, onion, crumbs, salt, allspice and pepper. Add meat; mix well, chill. Shape meat mixture into 1-in. balls.

2. In large skillet, brown meatballs in butter. Dissolve bouillon in boiling water; pour over meatballs and bring to boil over medium heat. Cover; simmer for 15 minutes.

3. Meanwhile, blend together cold water and flour. Remove meatballs from skillet, skim fat from pan juices and reserve juices. Stir 1 cup evaporated milk and flour/water mixture into pan juices in skillet; cook, uncovered, over low heat, stirring until sauce thickens.

4. Return meatballs to skillet. Stir in lemon juice. Serve with cooked noodles that have been tossed with poppy seeds and butter.

SWEET SAUSAGE ROLLS

Pigs in a blanket is one of those appetizers that's hard to stop eating. I've made these several times and everyone who tastes them thinks they're addicting!

—**LORI CABUNO** CANFIELD, OH

PREP: 25 MIN. • **BAKE:** 15 MIN.
MAKES: 2 DOZEN

- **1 tube (8 ounces) refrigerated crescent rolls**
- **24 miniature smoked sausage links**
- **½ cup butter, melted**
- **½ cup chopped nuts**
- **3 tablespoons honey**
- **3 tablespoons brown sugar**

1. Unroll crescent dough and separate into triangles; cut each lengthwise into three triangles. Place sausages on wide end of triangles; roll up tightly.

2. Combine the remaining ingredients in an 11x7-in. baking dish. Arrange sausage rolls, seam side down, in butter mixture. Bake, uncovered, at 400° for 15-20 minutes or until golden brown.

PEANUT SHRIMP KABOBS

Soy sauce and peanut butter are combined in a sauce that nicely glazes grilled shrimp.
—**HELEN GILDEN** MIDDLETOWN, DE

START TO FINISH: 20 MIN.
MAKES: 8 SERVINGS

- ¼ **cup sugar**
- ¼ **cup reduced-sodium soy sauce**
- ¼ **cup reduced-fat creamy peanut butter**
- 1 **tablespoon water**
- 1 **tablespoon canola oil**
- 3 **garlic cloves, minced**
- 1½ **pounds uncooked medium shrimp, peeled and deveined**

1. In a small saucepan, combine the first six ingredients until smooth. Cook and stir over medium-low heat until blended and sugar is dissolved. Set aside 6 tablespoons sauce.
2. On eight metal or soaked wooden skewers, thread the shrimp. Brush with remaining peanut sauce. Using long-handled tongs, moisten a paper towel with cooking oil and lightly coat the grill rack.
3. Grill kabobs, covered, over medium heat or broil 4 in. from the heat for 4-6 minutes or until shrimp turn pink, turning once. Brush with reserved sauce before serving.

CRAB RANGOON

Bite into these golden appetizers and you'll find a creamy crab filling that rivals restaurant fare. Best of all, these crowd-pleasers are baked instead of deep-fried, so they can be enjoyed without guilt.
—*TASTE OF HOME* TEST KITCHEN

START TO FINISH: 25 MIN.
MAKES: 14 APPETIZERS

- 3 **ounces reduced-fat cream cheese**
- ⅛ **teaspoon garlic salt**
- ⅛ **teaspoon Worcestershire sauce**
- ½ **cup lump crabmeat, drained**
- 1 **green onion, chopped**
- 14 **wonton wrappers**

1. In a small bowl, combine the cream cheese, garlic salt and Worcestershire sauce until smooth. Stir in crab and onion. Place 2 teaspoonfuls in the center of each wonton wrapper. Moisten edges with water; bring corners to center over filling and press edges together to seal.
2. Place on a baking sheet coated with cooking spray. Lightly spray wontons with cooking spray. Bake at 425° for 8-10 minutes or until golden brown. Serve warm.

QUICK BITES

_____   _____
_____   _____
_____   _____
_____   _____
_____   _____
_____   _____

CORN FRITTERS WITH CARAMELIZED ONION JAM

A friend's husband, who's a chef, made these light and fluffy fritters and paired them with a sweet-tart jam. I would never ask a chef to divulge his secrets, so I created my own version.

—**KIM CUPO** STAUNTON, VA

PREP: 30 MIN. • **COOK:** 15 MIN.
MAKES: 2 DOZEN (¾ CUP JAM)

- 1 **large sweet onion, halved and thinly sliced**
- 1 **tablespoon olive oil**
- 2 **teaspoons balsamic vinegar**
- ⅓ **cup apple jelly**
- ⅓ **cup canned diced tomatoes**
- 1 **tablespoon tomato paste**
- ⅛ **teaspoon curry powder**
- ⅛ **teaspoon ground cinnamon**
  Dash salt and pepper

FRITTERS

- 2 **cups biscuit/baking mix**
- 1 **can (11 ounces) gold and white corn, drained**
- 2 **eggs, lightly beaten**
- ½ **cup 2% milk**
- ½ **cup sour cream**
- ½ **teaspoon salt**
  Oil for frying

1. In a small skillet, saute onion in oil until golden brown. Add vinegar; cook and stir for 2-3 minutes. Set aside.

2. In a small saucepan, combine the jelly, tomatoes, tomato paste, curry powder, cinnamon, salt and pepper. Cook over medium heat for 5-7 minutes or until heated through. Add onion mixture. Cook and stir for 3 minutes; set aside and keep warm.

3. In a small bowl, combine the baking mix, corn, eggs, milk, sour cream and salt just until combined.

4. In a deep-fat fryer or electric skillet, heat oil to 375°. Drop batter by heaping tablespoonfuls, a few at a time, into hot oil; fry for 1½ minutes on each side or until golden brown. Drain on paper towels. Serve warm with jam.

GREEK PIZZAS

Customizable pita pizzas are a great way to please the whole family. Use a variety of veggies and cheeses to change things up.

—**DORIS ALLERS** PORTAGE, MI

START TO FINISH: 30 MIN.
MAKES: 4 SERVINGS

- 4 **pita breads (6 inches)**
- 1 **cup reduced-fat ricotta cheese**
- ½ **teaspoon garlic powder**
- 1 **package (10 ounces) frozen chopped spinach, thawed and squeezed dry**
- 3 **medium tomatoes, sliced**
- ¾ **cup crumbled feta cheese**
- ¾ **teaspoon dried basil**

1. Place pita breads on a baking sheet. Combine ricotta cheese and garlic powder; spread over pitas. Top with spinach, tomatoes, feta cheese and basil.

2. Bake at 400° for 12-15 minutes or until bread is lightly browned.

BACON & FONTINA STUFFED MUSHROOMS

I call these my "piled high cheesy stuffed mushrooms." They're an extra-special finger food that go over well at any party.
—**TAMMY REX** NEW TRIPOLI, PA

PREP: 30 MIN. • **BAKE:** 10 MIN.
MAKES: 2 DOZEN

- 4 **ounces cream cheese, softened**
- 1 **cup (4 ounces) shredded fontina cheese**
- 8 **bacon strips, cooked and crumbled**
- 4 **green onions, chopped**
- ¼ **cup chopped oil-packed sun-dried tomatoes**
- 3 **tablespoons minced fresh parsley**
- 24 **large fresh mushrooms (about 1¼ pounds), stems removed**
- 1 **tablespoon olive oil**

1. Preheat oven to 425°. In a small bowl, mix the first six ingredients until blended. Arrange mushroom caps in a greased 15x10x1-in. baking pan, stem side up. Spoon about 1 tablespoon filling into each.

2. Drizzle tops with olive oil. Bake, uncovered, 9-11 minutes or until golden brown and mushrooms are tender.

Almond Cheddar
Appetizers

ALMOND CHEDDAR APPETIZERS

START TO FINISH: 25 MIN. • **MAKES:** ABOUT 4 DOZEN

- 1 **cup mayonnaise**
- 2 **teaspoons Worcestershire sauce**
- 1 **cup (4 ounces) shredded sharp cheddar cheese**
- 1 **medium onion, chopped**
- ¾ **cup slivered almonds, chopped**
- 6 **bacon strips, cooked and crumbled**
- 1 **loaf (1 pound) French bread**

1. In a bowl, combine the mayonnaise and Worcestershire sauce; stir in cheese, onion, almonds and bacon.

2. Cut bread into ½-in. slices; spread with cheese mixture. Cut slices in half; place on a greased baking sheet. Bake at 400° for 8-10 minutes or until bubbly.

FREEZE OPTION *Place unbaked appetizers in a single layer on a baking sheet; freeze for 1 hour. Remove from pan and store in an airtight container for up to 2 months. When ready to use, place thawed appetizers on a greased baking sheet. Bake at 400° for 10 minutes or until warm and bubbly.*

I always have a supply of these on hand in my freezer. If guests drop in, I just pull out a batch and reheat. You can serve them as a snack, for brunch or with a cup of soup for lunch.
—**LINDA THOMPSON** SOUTHAMPTON, ON

CROWD-PLEASING
SANDWICHES

MINI TERIYAKI TURKEY SANDWICHES

It's a breeze to prepare this pulled turkey simmered in a delicious teriyaki sauce using your slow cooker. Serve it on lightly toasted sweet dinner rolls.

—**AMANDA HOOP** SEAMAN, OH

PREP: 20 MIN. • **COOK:** 5½ HOURS
MAKES: 20 SERVINGS

- 2 **boneless skinless turkey breast halves (2 pounds each)**
- ⅔ **cup packed brown sugar**
- ⅔ **cup reduced-sodium soy sauce**
- ¼ **cup cider vinegar**
- 3 **garlic cloves, minced**
- 1 **tablespoon minced fresh gingerroot**
- ½ **teaspoon pepper**
- 2 **tablespoons cornstarch**
- 2 **tablespoons cold water**
- 20 **Hawaiian sweet rolls**
- 2 **tablespoons butter, melted**

1. Place turkey in a 5- or 6-qt. slow cooker. In a small bowl, combine brown sugar, soy sauce, vinegar, garlic, ginger and pepper; pour over turkey. Cook, covered, on low 5-6 hours or until the meat is tender.

2. Remove turkey from slow cooker. In a small bowl, mix cornstarch and cold water until smooth; gradually stir into cooking liquid. When cool enough to handle, shred meat with two forks and return meat to slow cooker. Cook, covered, on high 30-35 minutes or until sauce is thickened.

3. Preheat oven to 325°. Split rolls and brush cut sides with butter; place on an ungreased baking sheet, cut side up. Bake 8-10 minutes or until toasted and golden brown. Spoon ⅓ cup turkey mixture on roll bottoms. Replace tops.

SUMMER TEA SANDWICHES

These dainty finger sandwiches are perfect for casual picnics or luncheons. Tarragon-seasoned chicken complements cucumber and cantaloupe slices.

—*TASTE OF HOME* TEST KITCHEN

PREP: 45 MIN. • **BAKE:** 20 MIN. + COOLING
MAKES: 12 SERVINGS

- ½ **teaspoon dried tarragon**
- ½ **teaspoon salt, divided**
- ¼ **teaspoon pepper**
- 1 **pound boneless skinless chicken breasts**
- ½ **cup reduced-fat mayonnaise**
- 1 **tablespoon finely chopped red onion**
- 1 **teaspoon dill weed**
- ½ **teaspoon lemon juice**
- 24 **slices soft multigrain bread, crusts removed**
- 1 **medium cucumber, thinly sliced**
- ¼ **medium cantaloupe, cut into 12 thin slices**

1. Combine the tarragon, ¼ teaspoon salt and pepper; rub over chicken. Place on a baking sheet coated with cooking spray.

2. Bake at 350° for 20-25 minutes or until a thermometer reads 170°. Cool to room temperature; thinly slice.

chicken, cantaloupe and remaining bread. Cut sandwiches in half diagonally. Serve immediately.

SEAFOOD SALAD MINI CROISSANTS
The perfect combination of simple and elegant, lobster salad on a buttery croissant is a delicious sandwich alternative. You can make the filling a day in advance.
—ATHENA RUSSELL FLORENCE, SC

START TO FINISH: 25 MIN.
MAKES: 10 SERVINGS

- ½ **cup mayonnaise**
- 1 **tablespoon snipped fresh dill**
- 1 **tablespoon minced chives**
- 1 **tablespoon lemon juice**
- ½ **teaspoon salt**
- ¼ **teaspoon pepper**
- ½ **pound imitation lobster**
- ½ **pound cooked small shrimp, peeled and deveined and coarsely chopped**
- 10 **miniature croissants, split**

1. In a large bowl, combine the mayonnaise, dill, chives, lemon juice, salt and pepper. Stir in lobster and shrimp. Cover and refrigerate until serving. Serve on croissants.
2. In a small bowl, combine the mayonnaise, onion, dill, lemon juice and remaining salt; spread over 12 bread slices. Top with cucumber,

CHIPOTLE SLIDERS
This recipe is the ultimate fast-fix mini burger and boasts fabulous flavor. Creamy mayo, cheese and sweet Hawaiian rolls tame the heat of the chipotle peppers.
—SHAWN SINGLETON VIDOR, TX

START TO FINISH: 30 MIN.
MAKES: 10 SLIDERS

- 1 **package (12 ounces) Hawaiian sweet rolls, divided**
- 1 **teaspoon salt**
- ½ **teaspoon pepper**
- 8 **teaspoons minced chipotle peppers in adobo sauce, divided**
- 1½ **pounds ground beef**
- 10 **slices pepper Jack cheese**
- ½ **cup mayonnaise**

1. Place 2 rolls in a food processor; process until crumbly. Transfer to a large bowl; add the salt, pepper and 6 teaspoons chipotle peppers. Crumble beef over mixture and mix well. Shape into 10 patties.
2. Grill burgers, covered, over medium heat for 3-4 minutes on each side or until a thermometer reads 160° and juices run clear. Top with cheese. Grill 1 minute longer or until cheese is melted.
3. Split remaining rolls and grill, cut side down, over medium heat for 30-60 seconds or until toasted. Combine mayonnaise and remaining chipotle peppers; spread over roll bottoms. Top each with a burger. Replace roll tops.

CHICKEN SALAD PARTY SANDWICHES

My famous chicken salad arrives at the party chilled in a plastic container. When it's time to set out the food, I stir in the pecans and assemble the sandwiches. They're great for buffet-style potlucks.

—**TRISHA KRUSE** EAGLE, ID

START TO FINISH: 20 MIN.
MAKES: 15 SERVINGS

- 4 cups cubed cooked chicken breast
- 1½ cups dried cranberries
- 2 celery ribs, finely chopped
- 2 green onions, thinly sliced
- ¼ cup chopped sweet pickles
- 1 cup fat-free mayonnaise
- ½ teaspoon curry powder
- ¼ teaspoon coarsely ground pepper
- ½ cup chopped pecans, toasted
- 15 whole wheat dinner rolls
  Torn leaf lettuce

1. In a large bowl, combine the first five ingredients. In a small bowl, combine the mayonnaise, curry and pepper. Add to chicken mixture; toss to coat. Chill until serving.

2. Stir pecans into chicken salad. Serve on rolls lined with lettuce.

STATE FAIR SUBS

PREP: 20 MIN. • **BAKE:** 20 MIN.
MAKES: 6 SERVINGS

- 1 loaf (1 pound unsliced) French bread
- 2 eggs
- ¼ cup milk
- ½ teaspoon pepper
- ¼ teaspoon salt
- 1 pound bulk Italian sausage
- 1½ cups chopped onion
- 2 cups (8 ounces) shredded part-skim mozzarella cheese

1. Cut bread in half lengthwise; carefully hollow out top and bottom of loaf, leaving a 1-in. shell. Cube removed bread. In a large bowl, beat the eggs, milk, pepper and salt. Add bread cubes and toss to coat; set aside.

2. In a skillet over medium heat, cook sausage and onion until the meat is no longer pink; drain. Add to the bread mixture. Spoon filling into bread shells; sprinkle with cheese. Wrap each in foil. Bake at 400° for 20-25 minutes or until the cheese is melted. Cut French bread into serving-size slices.

My college roommate and I tried these meaty subs at the Iowa State Fair. After a little experimenting, we re-created the recipe. We serve these to friends or eat them between classes.

—CHRISTI ROSS MILL CREEK, OK

ITALIAN SAUSAGE

When a Taste of Home recipe calls for Italian sausage, it is referring to sweet Italian sausage. Recipes using hot Italian sausage specifically call for that type.

PARTY PITAS

These mini pita wedges are easy to assemble using convenient store-bought ingredients. Greek vinaigrette and olives give them a Mediterranean flair.

—AWYNNE THURSTENSON
SILOAM SPRINGS, AR

START TO FINISH: 25 MIN.
MAKES: 2 DOZEN

- 4 whole wheat pita pocket halves
- ⅓ cup Greek vinaigrette
- ½ pound thinly sliced deli turkey
- 1 jar (7½ ounces) roasted sweet red peppers, drained and patted dry
- 2 cups fresh baby spinach
- 24 pitted Greek olives
- 24 frilled toothpicks

1. Brush insides of pita pockets with vinaigrette; fill with turkey, peppers and spinach. Cut each pita into six wedges.
2. Thread olives onto toothpicks; use to secure wedges.

BAJA CHICKEN & SLAW SLIDERS

Your guests will be asking for seconds after they take a bite into these Southwestern sliders, featuring a flavorful lime sauce and colorful, crunchy slaw. Control the heat by using more or less of the jalapenos or select mild, medium or hot chili powder.

—JANET HYNES MT. PLEASANT, WI

PREP: 30 MIN. • **GRILL:** 10 MIN.
MAKES: 8 SERVINGS

- ¼ cup reduced-fat sour cream
- ½ teaspoon grated lime peel
- ¼ teaspoon lime juice

SLAW
- 1 cup broccoli coleslaw mix
- 2 tablespoons finely chopped sweet red pepper
- 2 tablespoons finely chopped sweet onion
- 2 tablespoons minced fresh cilantro
- 2 teaspoons finely chopped seeded jalapeno pepper
- 2 teaspoons lime juice
- 1 teaspoon sugar

SLIDERS
- 4 boneless skinless chicken breast halves (4 ounces each)
- ½ teaspoon ground cumin
- ½ teaspoon chili powder
- ¼ teaspoon salt
- ¼ teaspoon coarsely ground pepper
- 8 Hawaiian sweet rolls, split
- 8 small lettuce leaves
- 8 slices tomato

1. In a small bowl, combine sour cream, lime peel and lime juice. In another small bowl, combine slaw ingredients. Chill sauce and slaw until serving.
2. Cut each chicken breast in half widthwise; flatten to ½-in. thickness. Sprinkle with seasonings.
3. Moisten a paper towel with cooking oil; using long-handled tongs, rub on grill rack to coat lightly. Grill chicken, covered, over medium heat or broil 4 in. from heat 4 to 7 minutes on each side or until no longer pink.
4. Grill rolls, cut sides down, 30-60 seconds or until toasted. Serve grilled chicken on rolls with lettuce, tomato, sauce and slaw.
NOTE *Wear disposable gloves when cutting hot peppers; the oils can burn skin. Avoid touching your face.*

ONION BEEF AU JUS

Garlic, sweet onions and soy sauce make a flavorful dipping juice for this hot, savory appetizer bread. The seasoned beef is delicious on cold sandwiches, too.

—MARILYN BROWN WEST UNION, IA

PREP: 20 MIN. • **BAKE:** 2½ HOURS + STANDING
MAKES: 12 SERVINGS

- 1 beef rump roast or bottom round roast (4 pounds)
- 2 tablespoons canola oil
- 2 large sweet onions, cut into ¼-inch slices
- 6 tablespoons butter, softened, divided
- 5 cups water
- ½ cup reduced-sodium soy sauce
- 1 envelope onion soup mix
- 1 garlic clove, minced
- 1 teaspoon browning sauce, optional
- 1 loaf (1 pound) French bread
- 1 cup (4 ounces) shredded Swiss cheese

1. In a Dutch oven over medium-high heat, brown roast on all sides in oil; drain. In a large skillet, saute onions in 2 tablespoons of butter until tender. Add the water, soy sauce, soup mix, garlic and, if desired, browning sauce. Pour over roast.

2. Cover and bake at 325° for 2½ hours or until meat is tender.

3. Let meat stand for 10 minutes, then thinly slice. Return meat to pan juices. Split bread lengthwise; cut into 3-in. sections. Spread with remaining butter. Place on a baking sheet.

4. Broil bread 4-6 in. from the heat for 2-3 minutes or until golden brown. Top with the beef and onions; sprinkle with cheese. Broil for 1-2 minutes or until the cheese is melted. Serve the bread with pan juices.

Onion Beef au Jus

HAWAIIAN BEEF SLIDERS

These dynamite burgers are packed with sweet and savory flavor and just a hint of heat. Pineapple and bacon may sound like an unusual combination, but you'll find they're the perfect match.

—MARY RELYEA CANASTOTA, NY

PREP: 30 MIN. + MARINATING
GRILL: 10 MIN. • **MAKES:** 6 SERVINGS

- 1 **can (20 ounces) unsweetened crushed pineapple**
- 1 **teaspoon pepper**
- ¼ **teaspoon salt**
- 1½ **pounds lean ground beef (90% lean)**
- ¼ **cup reduced-sodium soy sauce**
- 2 **tablespoons ketchup**
- 1 **tablespoon white vinegar**
- 2 **garlic cloves, minced**
- ¼ **teaspoon crushed red pepper flakes**
- 18 **miniature whole wheat buns**
  Baby spinach leaves
- 3 **center-cut bacon strips, cooked and crumbled**
  Sliced jalapeno peppers, optional

1. Drain pineapple, reserving juice and 1½ cups pineapple (save remaining pineapple for another use). In a large bowl, combine ¾ cup reserved crushed pineapple, pepper and salt. Crumble beef over mixture and mix well. Shape into 18 patties; place in two 11x7-in. dishes.

2. In a small bowl, combine soy sauce, ketchup, vinegar, garlic, pepper flakes and reserved pineapple juice. Pour half of marinade into each dish; cover and refrigerate 1 hour, turning once.

3. Drain and discard marinade. Moisten a paper towel with cooking oil; using long-handled tongs, coat grill rack lightly.

4. Grill patties, covered, over medium heat or broil 4 in. from heat 4-5 minutes on each side or until a thermometer reads 160° and juices run clear.

5. Grill buns, uncovered, 1-2 minutes or until toasted. Serve burgers on buns with spinach, remaining pineapple, bacon and jalapeno peppers if desired.

TUNA TEA SANDWICHES

A friend brought tuna sandwiches to a picnic years ago. I never got the recipe from her, but these are close and just as delicious. The addition of goat cheese and basil makes them extra special.

—LISA SNEED BAYFIELD, CO

START TO FINISH: 10 MIN.
MAKES: 4 TEA SANDWICHES

- 1 can (6 ounces) light water-packed tuna, drained and flaked
- 1 to 2 tablespoons mayonnaise
- ¼ teaspoon lemon-pepper seasoning
- 4 tablespoons crumbled goat cheese
- 4 slices multigrain bread, crusts removed
- 4 large fresh basil leaves

In a small bowl, combine the tuna, mayonnaise and lemon-pepper. Spread 1 tablespoon of goat cheese on each slice of bread. Spread two slices with tuna mixture; top with basil leaves and remaining bread. Cut in half or into desired shapes.

MINI MUFFULETTA

Mediterranean meets comfort food when French rolls are slathered with olive spread and stuffed with layers of salami and cheese. You can make these muffulettas the night before and cut them into appetizer-sized slices just before serving.

—GARETH CRANER MINDEN, NV

PREP: 25 MIN. + CHILLING
MAKES: 3 DOZEN

- 1 jar (10 ounces) pimiento-stuffed olives, drained and chopped
- 2 cans (4¼ ounces each) chopped ripe olives
- 2 tablespoons balsamic vinegar
- 1 tablespoon red wine vinegar
- 1 tablespoon olive oil
- 3 garlic cloves, minced
- 1 teaspoon dried basil
- 1 teaspoon dried oregano
- 6 French rolls, split
- ½ pound thinly sliced hard salami
- ¼ pound sliced provolone cheese
- ½ pound thinly sliced cotto salami
- ¼ pound sliced part-skim mozzarella cheese

1. In a large bowl, combine the first eight ingredients; set aside. Hollow out tops and bottoms of rolls, leaving ¾-in. shells (discard removed bread or save for another use).

2. Spread olive mixture over tops and bottoms of rolls. On roll bottoms, layer with hard salami, provolone cheese, cotto salami and mozzarella cheese. Replace tops.

3. Wrap tightly in plastic wrap. Refrigerate overnight. Cut each into six wedges; secure with toothpicks.

ANTIPASTO-STUFFED BAGUETTES

These Italian-style sandwiches can be served as an appetizer or as a light lunch.

—DIANNE HOLMGREN PRESCOTT, AZ

PREP: 25 MIN. + CHILLING • **BAKE:** 20 MIN.
MAKES: 2 DOZEN

- 1 can (2¼ ounces) sliced ripe olives, drained
- 2 tablespoons olive oil
- 1 teaspoon lemon juice
- 1 garlic clove, minced
- ⅛ teaspoon each dried basil, thyme, marjoram and rosemary, crushed
- 2 French bread baguettes (10½ ounces each)
- 1 package (4 ounces) crumbled feta cheese
- ½ pound thinly sliced Genoa salami
- 1 cup fresh baby spinach
- 1 jar (7¼ ounces) roasted red peppers, drained and chopped
- 1 can (14 ounces) water-packed artichoke hearts, rinsed, drained and quartered

1. In a blender, combine olives, oil, lemon juice, garlic and herbs; cover and process until olives are chopped. Set aside ⅓ cup olive mixture (refrigerate remaining mixture for another use).

2. Cut the top third off each baguette; carefully hollow out bottoms, leaving a ¼-in. shell (discard removed bread or save for another use).

3. Spread olive mixture in the bottom of each loaf. Sprinkle with feta cheese. Fold salami slices in half and place over cheese. Top with the spinach, red peppers and artichokes, pressing down as necessary. Replace bread tops. Wrap loaves tightly in foil. Refrigerate for at least 3 hours or overnight.

4. Serve cold, or to serve warm, preheat oven 350°. Place foil-wrapped loaves on a baking sheet. Bake 20-25 minutes or until heated through. Cut into slices; secure with a toothpick.

NOTE ⅓ cup purchased tapenade (olive paste) may be substituted for the olive mixture.

DELI SANDWICH PARTY PLATTER

Four kinds of meat, two kinds of spread and an assortment of breads add up to delicious sammies guests can assemble themselves.

—TASTE OF HOME TEST KITCHEN

START TO FINISH: 30 MIN.
MAKES: 24 SERVINGS

- 1 bunch green leaf lettuce
- 2 pounds sliced deli turkey
- 2 pounds sliced deli roast beef
- 1 pound sliced deli ham
- 1 pound thinly sliced hard salami
- 2 cartons (7 ounces each) roasted red pepper hummus
- 2 cartons (6½ ounces each) garden vegetable cheese spread
  Assorted breads and mini bagels

Arrange lettuce leaves on a serving platter; top with deli meats, rolled up if desired. Serve with hummus, cheese spread, breads and bagels.

EASY EXTRAS

Round out a party platter meal with fresh fruit, veggies and a store-bought dip or dessert. For ease, buy fruits or veggies that are ready to serve.

HAM 'N' CHEESE BISCUIT STACKS

These finger sandwiches are a pretty addition to any spread, yet filling enough to satisfy hearty appetites. I serve them at showers, tailgates and holiday parties.
—**KELLY WILLIAMS** FORKED RIVER, NJ

PREP: 1 HOUR • **BAKE:** 10 MIN. + COOLING
MAKES: 40 APPETIZERS

- 2 **tubes (12 ounces each) refrigerated buttermilk biscuits**
- ¾ **cup stone-ground mustard, divided**
- ½ **cup butter, softened**
- ¼ **cup chopped green onions**
- ¼ **cup mayonnaise**
- ¼ **cup honey**
- 10 **thick slices deli ham**
- 10 **slices Swiss cheese**
- 2½ **cups shredded romaine**
- 40 **frilled toothpicks**
- 20 **pitted ripe olives, drained and patted dry**
- 20 **pimiento-stuffed olives, drained and patted dry**

1. Preheat oven to 400°. Cut each biscuit in half, forming half circles. Place 2 in. apart on ungreased baking sheets. Spread each with ½ teaspoon mustard. Bake 8-10 minutes or until golden brown. Remove from pans to wire racks to cool.

2. In a small bowl, combine butter and onions. In another bowl, combine mayonnaise, honey and remaining mustard. Cut each slice of ham into four rectangles; cut each slice of cheese into four triangles.

3. Split each biscuit in half; spread bottom halves with butter mixture. Layer with one ham piece, one cheese piece and 1 tablespoon romaine on each biscuit bottom.

4. Spread mustard mixture over biscuit tops; place over romaine. Thread toothpicks through olives; insert into stacks. Refrigerate leftovers.

Feta Bruschetta

COOL &
TASTY

FETA BRUSCHETTA

You won't believe the compliments you'll receive when you greet guests with these appetizers. Each crispy bite offers the savory tastes of feta cheese, tomatoes, basil and garlic.

—**STACEY RINEHART** EUGENE, OR

START TO FINISH: 30 MIN.
MAKES: 10 APPETIZERS

- ¼ **cup butter, melted**
- ¼ **cup olive oil**
- 10 **slices French bread (1 inch thick)**
- 1 **package (4 ounces) crumbled feta cheese**
- 2 **to 3 garlic cloves, minced**
- 1 **tablespoon minced fresh basil or 1 teaspoon dried basil**
- 1 **large tomato, seeded and chopped**

1. In a small bowl, combine butter and oil; brush onto both sides of bread. Place on a baking sheet. Bake at 350° for 8-10 minutes or until lightly browned on top.
2. Combine the feta cheese, garlic and basil; sprinkle over toast. Top with tomato.

LEFTOVER FRENCH BREAD

If you have leftover French bread, slice the remainder, return it to its original wrapper, then place it in a plastic bag in the freezer. To use, dampen a microwave-safe paper towel, wrap it around the number of slices you'd like, and warm in the microwave for about 30 seconds.

CITRUS SPICED OLIVES

Lemon, lime and orange bring a burst of sunny citrus flavor to marinated olives. You can even blend the olives and spread the mixture onto baguette slices. Set them out for snacking at holiday buffets.

—**ANN SHEEHY** LAWRENCE, MA

PREP: 20 MIN. + CHILLING
MAKES: 4 CUPS

- ½ **cup white wine**
- ¼ **cup canola oil**
- 3 **tablespoons salt-free seasoning blend**
- 4 **garlic cloves, minced**
- ½ **teaspoon crushed red pepper flakes**
- 2 **teaspoons each grated orange, lemon and lime peels**
- 3 **tablespoons each orange, lemon and lime juices**
- 4 **cups mixed pitted olives**

In a large bowl, combine the first five ingredients. Add citrus peels and juices; whisk until blended. Add olives and toss to coat. Refrigerate, covered, at least 4 hours before serving.

HERB & ROASTED PEPPER CHEESECAKE

Roasted red peppers and fresh herbs add notes of sweetness, licorice and a peppery finish. Add a drizzle of oil just before serving, and pass the pita chips.

—LAURA JULIAN AMANDA, OH

PREP: 20 MIN. • **BAKE:** 35 MIN. + CHILLING
MAKES: 24 SERVINGS

- 3 packages (8 ounces each) cream cheese, softened
- ¾ cup whole-milk ricotta cheese
- 1½ teaspoons salt
- ¾ teaspoon pepper
- 3 eggs, lightly beaten
- 1½ cups roasted sweet red peppers, drained and finely chopped
- ¾ cup minced fresh basil
- ⅓ cup minced fresh chives
- 3 tablespoons minced fresh thyme
- 3 tablespoons crumbled cooked bacon
- 3 garlic cloves, minced
- 1 tablespoon olive oil
  Roasted sweet red pepper strips and additional minced chives, optional
  Baked pita chips

1. Preheat oven to 350°. Place a greased 9-in. springform pan on a double thickness of heavy-duty foil (about 18 in. square). Securely wrap foil around pan.

2. Place cream cheese, ricotta cheese, salt and pepper in a food processor; cover and process until smooth. Add eggs; pulse just until combined. Add red peppers, herbs, bacon and garlic; cover and pulse just until blended. Pour filling into prepared pan. Place springform pan in a large baking pan; add 1 in. of boiling water to larger pan.

3. Bake 35-45 minutes or until center is just set and top appears dull. Remove springform pan from water bath; remove foil. Cool cheesecake on a wire rack 10 minutes; loosen edges from pan with a knife. Cool 1 hour longer. Refrigerate overnight.

4. Remove rim from pan. Just before serving, drizzle cheesecake with oil; top with red pepper strips and chives if desired. Serve with pita chips.

MAKE-AHEAD MARINATED SHRIMP

Dress up your holiday buffet table with this tasty and easy-to-make shrimp recipe.

—PHYLLIS SCHMALZ KANSAS CITY, KS

PREP: 15 MIN. + MARINATING
MAKES: 6 CUPS

- ¾ cup water
- ½ cup red wine vinegar
- ¼ cup olive oil
- ¾ teaspoon salt
- ¾ teaspoon minced fresh oregano or ¼ teaspoon dried oregano
- ¾ teaspoon minced fresh thyme or ¼ teaspoon dried thyme
- 1 garlic clove, minced
- ¼ teaspoon pepper
- 1½ pounds peeled and deveined cooked jumbo shrimp
- 1 can (14 ounces) water-packed artichoke hearts, rinsed, drained and halved
- ½ pound small fresh mushrooms, halved

In a large resealable plastic bag, combine the first eight ingredients. Add the shrimp, artichokes and mushrooms; seal and turn to coat. Refrigerate for eight hours or overnight, turning occasionally.

Make-Ahead
Marinated Shrimp

HORSERADISH HAM CUBES

Horseradish and ham have always been perfect partners. Here they meet up for a zesty variation of classic ham roll-ups.

—CONNIE TOLLEY OAK HILL, WV

PREP: 15 MIN. + CHILLING
MAKES: ABOUT 5 DOZEN

- **1** **package (8 ounces) cream cheese, softened**
- **2** **tablespoons prepared horseradish**
- **1** **teaspoon Worcestershire sauce**
- **½** **teaspoon seasoned salt**
- **⅛** **teaspoon pepper**
- **10** **square slices deli ham**

1. In a small bowl, beat the cream cheese, horseradish, Worcestershire sauce, seasoned salt and pepper.
2. Set aside 2 ham slices; spread about 2 tablespoons cream cheese mixture over each remaining slice. Make two stacks, using four ham slices for each; top each stack with reserved slices. Wrap each stack in plastic wrap; chill for 4 hours. Cut each stack into 1-in. cubes.

RYE PARTY PUFFS

These puffs are pretty enough for a wedding reception and hearty enough to snack on while watching football on television. A platterful of these will disappear even with a small group.

—**KELLY WILLIAMS** FORKED RIVER, NJ

PREP: 30 MIN. • **BAKE:** 20 MIN. + COOLING
MAKES: 4½ DOZEN

- 1 **cup water**
- ½ **cup butter, cubed**
- ½ **cup all-purpose flour**
- ½ **cup rye flour**
- 2 **teaspoons dried parsley flakes**
- ½ **teaspoon garlic powder**
- ¼ **teaspoon salt**
- 4 **eggs**
   Caraway seeds

CORNED BEEF FILLING

- 2 **packages (8 ounces each) cream cheese, softened**
- 2 **packages (2 ounces each) thinly sliced deli corned beef, chopped**
- ½ **cup mayonnaise**
- ¼ **cup sour cream**
- 2 **tablespoons minced chives**
- 2 **tablespoons diced onion**
- 1 **teaspoon spicy brown or horseradish mustard**
- ⅛ **teaspoon garlic powder**
- 10 **small pimiento-stuffed olives, chopped**

1. In a large saucepan over medium heat, bring water and butter to a boil. Add the flours, parsley, garlic powder and salt all at once; stir until a smooth balls forms. Remove from the heat; let stand for 5 minutes. Beat in eggs, one at a time. Beat until smooth.
2. Drop batter by rounded teaspoonfuls 2 in. apart onto greased baking sheets. Sprinkle with caraway. Bake at 400° for 18-20 minutes or until golden. Remove to wire racks. Immediately cut a slit in each puff to allow steam to escape; cool.
3. In a large bowl, combine the first eight filling ingredients. Stir in olives. Split puffs; add filling. Refrigerate.

QUICK BITES

_____   _____
_____   _____
_____   _____
_____   _____
_____   _____
_____   _____

CHICKEN SALAD CAPRESE

This flavorful salad and bread combo will get rave reviews—guaranteed!

—FRANCES PIETSCH FLOWER MOUND, TX

PREP: 40 MIN. • **BAKE:** 5 MIN.
MAKES: 8 CUPS SALAD
(6½ DOZEN CROSTINI)

- 2 **cups shredded rotisserie chicken**
- 1 **pound fresh mozzarella cheese, cubed**
- 2 **cups grape tomatoes, halved**
- 1 **can (14 ounces) water-packed artichoke hearts, rinsed, drained and coarsely chopped**
- ½ **cup pitted Greek olives, thinly sliced**
- ¼ **cup minced fresh basil**
- ¼ **cup olive oil**
- 2 **garlic cloves, minced**
- ½ **teaspoon salt**
- ½ **teaspoon coarsely ground pepper**

TOMATO CROSTINI
- 2 **French bread baguettes (10½ ounces each)**
- 4 **garlic cloves**
- 2 **small tomatoes**
- ¼ **cup olive oil**
- 1 **teaspoon salt**

1. In a large bowl, combine the first six ingredients. In a small bowl, whisk the oil, garlic, salt and pepper; drizzle over chicken mixture and toss to coat. Refrigerate until serving.

2. Cut baguettes into ½-in. slices. Place on ungreased baking sheets. Bake at 425° for 2-4 minutes or until lightly browned. Cut garlic in half lengthwise; rub over bread. Cut tomatoes into quarters; rub over bread. Brush with oil and sprinkle with salt. Bake 2-3 minutes longer or until crisp. Serve crostini with chicken salad.

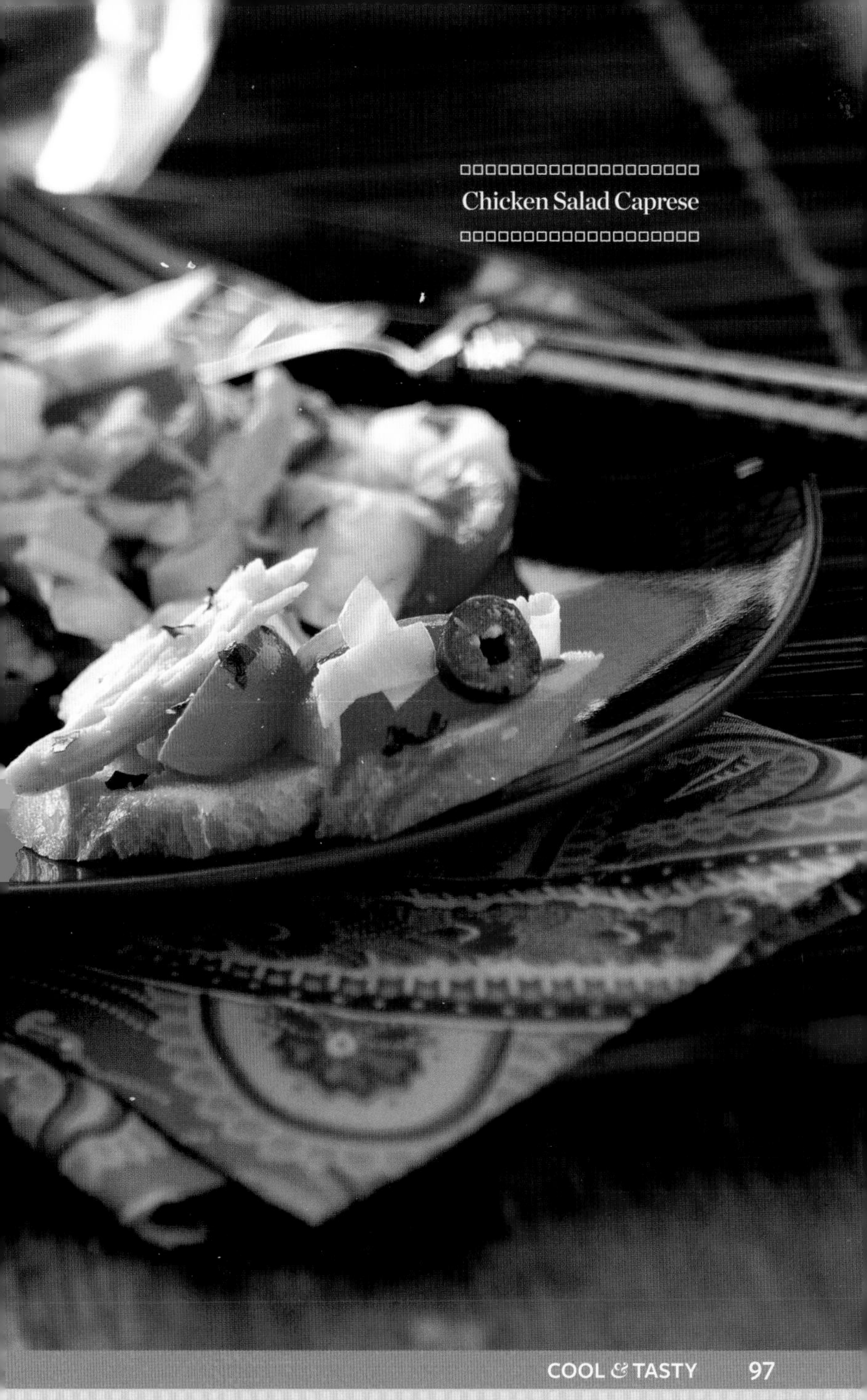

Chicken Salad Caprese

GARDEN SPRING ROLLS

My family loves Asian food, and this recipe captures the healthy benefits of the nutritious vegetables without any loss of vitamins from cooking. Even kids will gobble up raw veggies if you offer them in the form of a spring roll and give them a delicious dipping sauce.
—TERRI LYNN MERRITTS NASHVILLE, TN

START TO FINISH: 30 MIN.
MAKES: 8 SPRING ROLLS

- 3 **cups shredded cabbage or romaine lettuce**
- ¼ **cup Thai chili sauce**
- 8 **spring roll wrappers or rice papers (8 inches)**
- 1 **small sweet red pepper, thinly sliced**
- ½ **cup thinly sliced sweet onion**
- 1 **small ripe avocado, peeled and thinly sliced**
- 4 **fresh basil leaves, thinly sliced**
  Additional Thai chili sauce, optional

1. In a small bowl, mix cabbage and chili sauce. Fill a shallow bowl with water. Soak a spring roll wrapper in the water just until pliable, 30-45 seconds (depending on thickness of rice papers); remove wrapper from bowl, allowing excess water to drip off.

2. Place on a flat surface. Layer cabbage mixture, red pepper and onion down the center; top with avocado and basil. Fold both ends over filling; fold one long side over the filling, then roll up tightly. Place seam side down on a serving platter. Repeat with remaining ingredients.

3. Cover with damp paper towels until serving. Cut rolls diagonally in half. If desired, serve with additional Thai chili sauce.

HUEVOS DIABLOS

Tired of the same old ho-hum deviled eggs? Then you'll like these that feature a little bit of Mexican heat. If you prefer a milder version, remove the ribs and seeds from the jalapeno pepper.
—LINDA ROSS WILLIAMSPORT, PA

START TO FINISH: 30 MIN.
MAKES: 2 DOZEN

- 12 **hard-cooked eggs**
- 6 **tablespoons minced fresh cilantro, divided**
- 6 **tablespoons mayonnaise**
- 2 **green onions, thinly sliced**
- ¼ **cup sour cream**
- 1 **jalapeno pepper, seeded and minced**
- 1½ **teaspoons grated lime peel**
- 1 **teaspoon ground cumin**
- ¼ **teaspoon salt**
- ⅛ **teaspoon pepper**

Cut eggs in half lengthwise. Remove yolks; set whites aside. In a small bowl, mash yolks. Add 3 tablespoons cilantro, mayonnaise, onions, sour cream, jalapeno, lime peel, cumin, salt and pepper; mix well. Stuff or pipe into egg whites. Refrigerate until serving. Garnish with remaining cilantro.

CRAB CUCUMBER BITES

I look for recipes that are deceptively easy. These fancy-but-quick crab and cucumber appetizers are heavenly, and the stand-out colors light up any gathering or holiday table, no matter the season.

—NANCY CZARNICK DESERT HILLS, AZ

START TO FINISH: 30 MIN.
MAKES: 4 DOZEN

- **3 medium cucumbers**
- **⅔ cup reduced-fat cream cheese**
- **2 teaspoons lemon juice**
- **1 teaspoon hot pepper sauce**
- **1 package (8 ounces) imitation crabmeat, chopped**
- **⅓ cup finely chopped sweet red pepper**
- **2 green onions, sliced**

1. Peel strips from cucumbers to create striped edges; cut each cucumber into 16 slices, about ¼-in. thick. Pat dry with paper towels; set aside.

2. In a small bowl, beat the cream cheese, lemon juice and pepper sauce until smooth. Fold in the crab, red pepper and onions. Place 1 heaping teaspoonful onto each cucumber slice. Serve immediately.

Antipasto Platter

ANTIPASTO PLATTER

PREP: 10 MIN. + CHILLING • **MAKES:** 14-16 SERVINGS

- 1 jar (24 ounces) pepperoncini, drained
- 1 can (15 ounces) garbanzo beans or chickpeas, rinsed and drained
- 2 cups halved fresh mushrooms
- 2 cups halved cherry tomatoes
- ½ pound provolone cheese, cubed
- 1 can (6 ounces) pitted ripe olives, drained
- 1 package (3½ ounces) sliced pepperoni
- 1 bottle (8 ounces) Italian vinaigrette dressing
  Lettuce leaves

1. In a large bowl, combine pepperoncini, beans, mushrooms, tomatoes, cheese, olives and pepperoni. Pour vinaigrette over mixture; toss to coat.

2. Refrigerate at least 30 minutes or overnight. Arrange on a lettuce-lined platter. Serve with toothpicks.

> We entertain often, and antipasto is one of our favorite crowd-pleasers. Everyone loves having so many ingredients to nibble on. It's a satisfying change of pace from the usual chips and dip.
> —**TERI LINDQUIST** GURNEE, IL

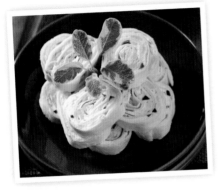

APPETIZER TORTILLA PINWHEELS

A friend gave me the recipe for this attractive and tasty appetizer. You can prepare the rolls in advance and slice into pinwheels just before serving.

—**PAT WAYMIRE** YELLOW SPRINGS, OH

PREP: 20 MIN. + CHILLING
MAKES: ABOUT 4 DOZEN

- 1 **cup (8 ounces) sour cream**
- 1 **package (8 ounces) cream cheese, softened**
- 1 **can (4¼ ounces) chopped ripe olives**
- 1 **can (4 ounces) chopped green chilies, well drained**
- 1 **cup (4 ounces) shredded cheddar cheese**
- ½ **cup chopped green onions**
  Garlic powder to taste
  Seasoned salt to taste
- 5 **flour tortillas (10 inches), room temperature**
  Fresh parsley for garnish
  Salsa

1. In a large bowl, beat the first eight ingredients until blended. Spread over the tortillas; roll up tightly. Wrap each with plastic wrap, twisting ends; refrigerate for several hours. Unwrap; cut into ½-in. to ¾-in. slices. (An electric knife works best.) Discard ends. Garnish with parsley. Serve with salsa if desired.

SMOKED SALMON CHERRY TOMATOES

These bright red festive bites are a showstopping finger food during the winter holidays, at Easter and the Fourth of July. With the smoked salmon filling, these appetizers are elegant but convenient because you can prepare them in advance.

—**PAT CRONIN** LAREDO, TX

START TO FINISH: 25 MIN.
MAKES: 2½ DOZEN

- 30 **cherry tomatoes**
- 3 **ounces smoked salmon or lox, finely chopped**
- ⅓ **cup finely chopped onion**
- ⅓ **cup finely chopped green pepper**
  Salt and pepper to taste
- 1 **package (3 ounces) cream cheese, softened**
- 1 **teaspoon milk**
  Fresh dill sprigs

1. Cut a thin slice off each tomato top; scoop out and discard pulp. Invert tomatoes on paper towels to drain. In a large bowl, combine the salmon, onion, green pepper, salt and pepper. Spoon into tomatoes.

2. In a small bowl, beat cream cheese and milk until smooth. Insert a star tip into a pastry or plastic bag. Pipe a small amount of cream cheese mixture onto tomatoes. Garnish with dill.

DELIGHTFUL DEVILED EGGS

The subtle flavors of mustard and onion make these deviled eggs a favorite at our house. Garnish each egg half with fresh parsley for a pretty presentation.
—**KELLY ALANIZ** EUREKA, CA

START TO FINISH: 20 MIN.
MAKES: 1 DOZEN

- **6 hard-cooked eggs**
- **2 tablespoons mayonnaise**
- **1½ teaspoons grated onion**
- **1½ teaspoons sweet pickle relish**
- **½ teaspoon spicy brown mustard**
- **¼ teaspoon salt**
- **⅛ teaspoon crushed red pepper flakes**
- **⅛ teaspoon pepper**

1. Slice eggs in half lengthwise. Remove yolks; set whites aside. In a small bowl, mash yolks. Stir in the mayonnaise, onion, relish, mustard, salt, pepper flakes and pepper.

2. Pipe or spoon into egg whites. Refrigerate until serving.

LIGHTENED-UP VEGGIE PIZZA SQUARES

This hearty, creamy and full-bodied veggie pizza, served as an appetizer, is sure to bring compliments from your guests.

—SANDRA SHAFER MOUNTAIN VIEW, CA

PREP: 30 MIN. + CHILLING
MAKES: 2 DOZEN

- 2 **tubes (8 ounces each) refrigerated reduced-fat crescent rolls**
- 1 **package (8 ounces) reduced-fat cream cheese**
- 1 **package (8 ounces) fat-free cream cheese**
- ½ **cup plain yogurt**
- ⅓ **cup reduced-fat mayonnaise**
- ¼ **cup fat-free milk**
- 1 **tablespoon dill weed**
- ½ **teaspoon garlic salt**
- 1 **cup shredded carrots**
- 1 **cup fresh cauliflowerets, chopped**
- 1 **cup fresh broccoli florets, chopped**
- 1 **cup julienned green pepper**
- 1 **cup sliced fresh mushrooms**
- 2 **cans (2¼ ounces each) sliced ripe olives, drained**
- ¼ **cup finely chopped sweet onion**

1. Unroll both tubes of crescent dough and pat into an ungreased 15x10x 1-in. baking pan; seal the seams and perforations. Bake at 375° for 10-12 minutes or until golden brown. Cool completely on a wire rack.

2. In a small bowl, beat the cream cheeses, yogurt, mayonnaise, milk, dill and garlic salt until smooth. Spread over crust. Sprinkle with carrots, cauliflower, broccoli, green pepper, mushrooms, olives and onion. Cover and refrigerate for at least 1 hour.

3. Cut into squares. Refrigerate leftovers.

ENSENADA SHRIMP COCKTAIL

Tomatoes, peppers, onions and cilantro replace traditional cocktail sauce in this lively Southwestern makeover of the popular shrimp appetizer.
—**TERI RASEY** CADILLAC, MI

PREP: 15 MIN. + CHILLING
MAKES: 8 SERVINGS

- 1 **pound peeled and deveined cooked medium shrimp**
- 2 **plum tomatoes, seeded and chopped**
- 3 **jalapeno peppers, seeded and chopped**
- 1 **serrano pepper, seeded and chopped**
- ¼ **cup chopped red onion**
- 2 **green onions, chopped**
- 2 **tablespoons minced fresh cilantro**
- 2 **tablespoons olive oil**
- 1 **tablespoon rice vinegar**
- 1 **tablespoon key lime juice or lime juice**
- 1 **teaspoon adobo seasoning**
  Lime wedges

1. In a large bowl, combine the shrimp, tomatoes, peppers, onions and cilantro. Combine the oil, vinegar, lime juice and seasoning; drizzle over shrimp mixture and toss to coat.

2. Refrigerate for at least 1 hour. Using a slotted spoon, place shrimp mixture in cocktail glasses, about ½ cup in each. Garnish with lime wedges.

NOTE *Wear disposable gloves when cutting hot peppers; the oils can burn skin. Avoid touching your face.*

APRICOT-RICOTTA STUFFED CELERY

This healthful, protein-rich filling can double as a dip for sliced apples. I often make it ahead so it's ready as an impromptu snack.
—**DOROTHY REINHOLD** MALIBU, CA

START TO FINISH: 15 MIN.
MAKES: ABOUT 2 DOZEN

- 3 **dried apricots**
- ½ **cup part-skim ricotta cheese**
- 2 **teaspoons brown sugar**
- ¼ **teaspoon grated orange peel**
- ⅛ **teaspoon salt**
- 5 **celery ribs, cut into 1½ inch pieces**

Place apricots in a food processor. Cover and process until finely chopped. Add the ricotta cheese, brown sugar, orange peel and salt; cover and process until blended. Stuff or pipe into celery. Chill until serving.

MOTHER LODE PRETZELS

PREP: 35 MIN. + STANDING • **MAKES:** 4½ DOZEN

- 1 package (10 ounces) pretzel rods
- 1 package (14 ounces) caramels
- 1 tablespoon evaporated milk
- 1¼ cups miniature semisweet chocolate chips
- 1 cup plus 2 tablespoons butterscotch chips
- ⅔ cup milk chocolate toffee bits
- ¼ cup chopped walnuts, toasted

1. With a sharp knife, cut pretzel rods in half; set aside. In a large saucepan over low heat, melt caramels with milk. In a large shallow bowl, combine the chips, toffee bits and walnuts.
2. Pour caramel mixture into a 2-cup glass measuring cup. Dip the cut end of each pretzel piece two-thirds of the way into caramel mixture (reheat in microwave if mixture becomes too thick for dipping). Allow excess caramel to drip off, then roll pretzels in the chip mixture. Place on waxed paper until set. Store in an airtight container.

> I brought these savory-sweet pretzels to a family gathering, and they disappeared from the dessert tray before dessert was even served! My family raves about how awesome they are.
> —**CARRIE BENNETT** MADISON, WI

Mother Lode Pretzels

VEGGIE HAM CRESCENT WREATH

Impress your guests with the look and flavor of this pretty crescent roll appetizer. The pineapple cream cheese adds a special sweet touch.

—DIXIE LUNDQUIST CHANDLER, AZ

PREP: 20 MIN. • **BAKE:** 15 MIN. + COOLING
MAKES: 16 APPETIZERS

- **2 tubes (8 ounces each) refrigerated crescent rolls**
- **½ cup spreadable pineapple cream cheese**
- **⅓ cup diced fully cooked ham**
- **¼ cup finely chopped sweet yellow pepper**
- **¼ cup finely chopped green pepper**
- **½ cup chopped fresh broccoli florets**
- **6 grape tomatoes, quartered**
- **1 tablespoon chopped red onion**

1. Remove crescent dough from tubes (do not unroll). Cut each roll into eight slices. Arrange in an 11-in. circle on an ungreased 14-in. pizza pan.

2. Bake at 375° for 15-20 minutes or until golden brown. Cool for 5 minutes before carefully removing to a serving platter; cool completely.

3. Spread cream cheese over wreath; top with ham, peppers, broccoli, tomatoes and onion. Store in the refrigerator.

CALIFORNIA ROLLS

This tastes as good as any restaurant or store-bought California roll. For best results, use sushi rice to ensure the right consistency.

—TASTE OF HOME TEST KITCHEN

PREP: 1 HOUR + STANDING
MAKES: 64 PIECES

- 2 **cups sushi rice, rinsed and drained**
- 2 **cups water**
- ¼ **cup rice vinegar**
- 2 **tablespoons sugar**
- ½ **teaspoon salt**
- 2 **tablespoons sesame seeds, toasted**
- 2 **tablespoons black sesame seeds**
  Bamboo sushi mat
- 8 **nori sheets**
- 1 **small cucumber, seeded and julienned**
- 3 **ounces imitation crabmeat, julienned**
- 1 **medium ripe avocado, peeled and julienned**
  Reduced-sodium soy sauce, prepared wasabi and pickled ginger slices, optional

1. In a large saucepan, combine rice and water; let stand for 30 minutes. Bring to a boil. Reduce heat to low; cover and simmer for 15-20 minutes or until water is absorbed and rice is tender. Remove from the heat. Let stand, covered, for 10 minutes.

2. Meanwhile, in small bowl, combine the vinegar, sugar and salt, stirring until sugar is dissolved.

3. Transfer rice to a large shallow bowl; drizzle with vinegar mixture. With a wooden paddle or spoon, stir rice with a slicing motion to cool slightly. Cover with a damp cloth to keep moist. (Rice mixture may be made up to 2 hours ahead and stored at room temperature, covered with a damp towel. Do not refrigerate.)

4. Sprinkle toasted and black sesame seeds onto a plate; set aside. Place sushi mat on a work surface so mat rolls away from you; line with plastic wrap. Place ¾ cup rice on plastic. With moistened fingers, press rice into an 8-in. square. Top with one nori sheet.

5. Arrange a small amount of cucumber, crab and avocado about 1½ in. from bottom edge of nori sheet. Roll up rice mixture over filling, using the bamboo mat to lift and compress the mixture while rolling; remove plastic wrap as you roll.

6. Remove mat; roll sushi rolls in sesame seeds. Cover with plastic wrap. Repeat with remaining ingredients to make eight rolls. Cut each into eight pieces. Serve with soy sauce, wasabi and ginger slices if desired.

CARAMEL APPLE AND BRIE SKEWERS

START TO FINISH: 10 MIN.
MAKES: 6 SKEWERS

- 2 medium apples, cubed
- 1 log (6 ounces) Brie cheese, cubed
- ½ cup hot caramel ice cream topping
- ½ cup finely chopped macadamia nuts
- 2 tablespoons dried cranberries

On each of six wooden appetizer skewers, alternately thread apple and cheese cubes; place on a serving tray. Drizzle with caramel topping; sprinkle with macadamia nuts and cranberries.

HONEY-NUT ENDIVE APPETIZERS

Sweet and savory flavors combine in this elegant appetizer. It's a nice light option to serve before a big meal.
—**CARMEL GILLOGLY** FORT MILL, SC

START TO FINISH: 10 MIN.
MAKES: 1 DOZEN

- ⅓ cup crumbled goat cheese
- ⅓ cup crumbled Gorgonzola cheese
- ⅓ cup pine nuts
- ⅓ cup chopped walnuts
- ⅓ cup golden raisins
- 4 bacon strips, cooked and crumbled
- 2 heads Belgian endive, separated into leaves
- ⅓ cup honey

In a small bowl, combine the first six ingredients. Spoon into endive leaves. Drizzle honey over cheese mixture. Serve immediately.

> I'm a caterer, and this is one of my best-selling appetizers. The shortcut of using prepared caramel makes these little gems a snap to prepare.
> —**CAMILLE ELLIS** TAMPA, FL

QUICK BITES

Caramel Apple and
Brie Skewers

THYME-SEA SALT CRACKERS

These homemade crackers are incredibly light and crispy. They are great on their own as a snack or top them with some sharp white cheddar.

—JESSICA WIRTH CHARLOTTE, NC

PREP: 25 MIN. • **BAKE:** 10 MIN./BATCH
MAKES: ABOUT 7 DOZEN

- 2½ **cups all-purpose flour**
- ½ **cup white whole wheat flour**
- 1 **teaspoon salt**
- ¾ **cup water**
- ¼ **cup plus 1 tablespoon olive oil, divided**
- 1 **to 2 tablespoons minced fresh thyme**
- ¾ **teaspoon sea or kosher salt**

1. Preheat oven to 375°. In a large bowl, whisk flours and salt. Gradually add water and ¼ cup oil, tossing with a fork until dough holds together when pressed. Divide dough into three portions. On a lightly floured surface, roll each portion of dough to ⅛-in. thickness. Cut with a floured 1½-in. round cookie cutter. Place 1-in. apart on ungreased baking sheets. Prick each cracker with a fork; brush lightly with remaining oil. Mix thyme and sea salt; sprinkle over crackers.

2. Bake 9-11 minutes or until bottoms are lightly browned.

SEAFOOD SALAD STUFFED SHELLS

This excellent appetizer is a favorite with my guests. It's cool, refreshing, easy to make and has a lovely seafood flavor. The green onions add a nice crunch.

—**SUZY HORVATH** MILWAUKIE, OR

PREP: 50 MIN. + CHILLING
MAKES: ABOUT 3 DOZEN

- 1 **package (12 ounces) jumbo pasta shells**
- 2 **packages (8 ounces each) cream cheese, softened**
- ⅓ **cup mayonnaise**
- 2 **teaspoons sugar**
- 1½ **teaspoons lemon juice**
- ⅛ **teaspoon salt**
- ⅛ **teaspoon coarsely ground pepper**
- ⅛ **teaspoon cayenne pepper**
- 3 **cans (6 ounces each) lump crabmeat, drained**
- ½ **pound frozen cooked salad shrimp, thawed**
- 12 **green onions, finely chopped**

1. Cook pasta according to package directions; drain and rinse in cold water. Cool to room temperature.

2. In a large bowl, combine the cream cheese, mayonnaise, sugar, lemon juice, salt, pepper and cayenne. Gently stir in the crab, shrimp and onions. Stuff shells, about 2 tablespoons in each. Cover and refrigerate for at least 1 hour.

BLUE CHEESE-STUFFED STRAWBERRIES

I was enjoying a salad with strawberries and blue cheese when the idea hit me to stuff the strawberries and serve them as an appetizer. It worked out perfectly, and the flavors blend nicely.

—**DIANE NEMITZ** LUDINGTON, MI

START TO FINISH: 25 MIN.
MAKES: 16 APPETIZERS

- ½ **cup balsamic vinegar**
- 3 **ounces fat-free cream cheese**
- ½ **cup crumbled blue cheese**
- 16 **large fresh strawberries**
- 3 **tablespoons finely chopped pecans, toasted**

1. Place vinegar in a small saucepan. Bring to a boil; cook until liquid is reduced by half. Cool to room temperature.

2. Meanwhile, in a small bowl, beat cream cheese until smooth. Beat in blue cheese. Remove stems and scoop out centers from strawberries; fill each with about 2 teaspoons cheese mixture. Sprinkle pecans over filling, pressing lightly. Chill until serving. Drizzle with balsamic vinegar.

Cucumber-Stuffed
Cherry Tomatoes

CUCUMBER-STUFFED CHERRY TOMATOES

START TO FINISH: 25 MIN. • **MAKES:** 2 DOZEN

- 24 **cherry tomatoes**
- 1 **package (3 ounces) cream cheese, softened**
- 2 **tablespoons mayonnaise**
- ¼ **cup finely chopped peeled cucumber**
- 1 **tablespoon finely chopped green onion**
- 2 **teaspoons minced fresh dill**

1. Cut a thin slice off the top of each tomato. Scoop out and discard pulp; invert tomatoes onto paper towels to drain.

2. In a small bowl, combine cream cheese and mayonnaise until smooth; stir in the cucumber, onion and dill. Spoon into tomatoes. Refrigerate until serving.

> This is a wonderful appetizer that you can make ahead. And it's the perfect use for your homegrown cherry tomatoes. I often triple the recipe because they disappear fast.
> —**CHRISTI MARTIN** ELKO, NV

TIERED CHEESE SLICES

This is my go-to appetizer for a party or potuck. I get requests for the recipe every time. The simple ingredients and pre-sliced cheddar cheese go together in minutes.
—**DIANE BENJAMINSON** COLEVILLE, , SK

PREP: 45 MIN. + CHILLING
MAKES: ABOUT 4 DOZEN

- 1 **package (8 ounces) cream cheese, softened**
- ½ **teaspoon hot pepper sauce**
- ¼ **teaspoon salt**
- ¼ **cup chopped pecans**
- ¼ **cup dried cranberries**
- 2 **packages (8 ounces each) deli-style cheddar cheese slices (about 3 inches square)**
  Assorted crackers

1. In a large bowl, combine the cream cheese, hot pepper sauce and salt. Stir in pecans and cranberries.

2. On a 12-in. square of aluminum foil, place two slices of cheese side by side; spread with 2-3 tablespoons cream cheese mixture. Repeat layers six times. Top with two cheese slices. (Save remaining cheese slices for another use.)

3. Fold foil around cheese and seal tightly. Refrigerate for 8 hours or overnight. Cut in half lengthwise and then widthwise into ¼-in. slices. Serve with crackers.

CRAB-STUFFED SNOW PEAS

These crunchy appetizers have a wonderful crabmeat flavor and make an attractive addition to your party platter. I love that they're simple to prepare.

—AGNES WARD STRATFORD, ON

START TO FINISH: 20 MIN.
MAKES: 16 APPETIZERS

- 1 can (6 ounces) crabmeat, drained, flaked and cartilage removed
- 2 tablespoons mayonnaise
- 1 tablespoon chili sauce or seafood cocktail sauce
- ⅛ teaspoon salt
- 3 drops hot pepper sauce
  Dash pepper
- 16 fresh snow peas

1. In small bowl, combine the crab, mayonnaise, chili sauce, salt, hot pepper sauce and pepper.

2. Place snow peas in a steamer basket; place in a small saucepan over 1 in. of water. Bring to a boil; cover and steam for 30 seconds for until softened. Drain and immediately place snow peas in ice water. Drain and pat dry.

3. With a sharp knife, split pea pods along the curved edges. Spoon 1 tablespoon of crab mixture into each. Refrigerate until serving.

IMITATION CRAB

Imitation crabmeat, most often made with Alaskan pollack, can be substituted for real crab in equal proportions in most recipes. The flavor and texture will be slightly different than the real thing.

CUCUMBER RYE SNACKS

We have lots of pig roasts here in Kentucky, and these mini cucumber sandwiches are the perfect nibblers to enjoy while the main course is roasting.

—REBECCA ROSE MT. WASHINGTON, KY

PREP: 20 MIN. + STANDING
MAKES: 2½ DOZEN

- 1 package (8 ounces) cream cheese, softened
- 2 tablespoons mayonnaise
- 2 teaspoons Italian salad dressing mix
- 30 slices snack rye bread
- 30 thin slices cucumber
  Fresh dill sprigs and chive blossoms

1. In a large bowl, beat the cream cheese, mayonnaise and dressing mix until blended. Let stand for 30 minutes.

2. Spread mixture on rye bread. Top each with a slice of cucumber, dill sprig and chive blossom. Cover and refrigerate until serving.

ASIAN TUNA BITES WITH DIJON DIPPING SAUCE

Folks love eating anything on a stick, and these quick, easy and fresh tuna bites always hit the spot. They're a snap to make and beautiful to serve. This recipe can be made ahead, and the tuna also tastes great when it's grilled.

—JAMIE BROWN-MILLER NAPA, CA

START TO FINISH: 30 MIN.
MAKES: 2½ DOZEN (½ CUP SAUCE)

- 3 **tablespoons Dijon mustard**
- 2 **tablespoons red wine vinegar**
- 2 **tablespoons reduced-sodium soy sauce**
- 1 **tablespoon sesame oil**
- 1 **teaspoon hot pepper sauce**
- 1 **pound tuna steaks, cut into thirty 1-inch cubes**
  Cooking spray
- ¼ **cup sesame seeds**
- ½ **teaspoon salt**
- ¼ **teaspoon pepper**
- 2 **green onions, finely chopped**

1. In a small bowl, whisk the first five ingredients; set aside. Spritz tuna with cooking spray. Sprinkle with sesame seeds, salt and pepper. In a large nonstick skillet, brown tuna on all sides in batches until medium-rare or slightly pink in the center; remove from the skillet.

2. On each of 30 wooden appetizer skewers, thread one tuna cube. Arrange on a serving platter. Garnish with onions. Serve with sauce.

Asian Tuna Bites with Dijon Dipping Sauce

MARINATED SAUSAGE KABOBS

PREP: 20 MIN. + MARINATING
MAKES: 3 DOZEN

- ¼ cup olive oil
- 1 tablespoon white vinegar
- ½ teaspoon minced garlic
- ½ teaspoon dried basil
- ½ teaspoon dried oregano
- 12 ounces cheddar cheese, cut into ¾-in. cubes
- 1 can (6 ounces) pitted ripe olives, drained
- 4 ounces hard salami, cut into ¾-in. cubes
- 1 medium sweet red pepper, cut into ¾-inch pieces
- 1 medium green pepper, cut into ¾-inch pieces

1. In a large resealable plastic bag, combine first five ingredients; add remaining ingredients. Seal bag and turn to coat; refrigerate at least 4 hours. Drain and discard marinade.

2. For each kabob, thread one piece each of cheese, olive, salami and pepper onto a toothpick.

These colorful appetizers are so fun they'll be the talk of the party. And they're easy to make. Simply assemble the day before and refrigerate until ready to serve.
—**JOANNE BOONE** DANVILLE, OH

SMOKED SALMON PINWHEELS

Want to wow guests without spending all day in the kitchen? Turn to this tasty and impressive recipe.

—CRISTINA MATHERS SAN MIGUEL, CA

START TO FINISH: 20 MIN.
MAKES: 32 APPETIZERS

- 1 **package (8 ounces) cream cheese, softened**
- 1 **tablespoon snipped fresh dill**
- 1 **tablespoon capers, drained**
- ½ **teaspoon garlic powder**
- ½ **teaspoon lemon juice**
- 4 **spinach tortillas (8 inches), room temperature**
- ½ **pound smoked salmon fillets, flaked**

1. In a small bowl, combine the cream cheese, dill, capers, garlic powder and lemon juice. Spread over tortillas; top with salmon. Roll up tightly.
2. Cut into 1-in. pieces; secure with toothpicks. Chill until serving. Discard toothpicks before serving. Refrigerate leftovers.

CHEESE STRAWS

It takes only a few on-hand ingredients to make these long, crisp cracker sticks. The hand-held snacks make for easy mingling at parties.

—ELIZABETH ROBINSON CONROE, TX

PREP: 20 MIN. • **BAKE:** 15 MIN. + COOLING
MAKES: 2½ DOZEN

- ½ **cup butter, softened**
- 2 **cups (8 ounces) shredded sharp cheddar cheese**
- 1¼ **cups all-purpose flour**
- ½ **teaspoon salt**
- ¼ **teaspoon cayenne pepper**

1. Preheat oven to 350°. In a large bowl, beat butter until light and fluffy. Beat in cheese until blended. Combine flour, salt and cayenne; stir into cheese mixture until a dough forms. Roll into a 15x6-in. rectangle. Cut into thirty 6-in. strips. Gently place strips 1 in. apart on ungreased baking sheets.
2. Bake 15-20 minutes or until lightly browned. Cool 5 minutes before removing from pans to wire racks to cool completely. Store straws in an airtight container.

CAPERS, DEFINED

Capers are the immature buds from a bush native to the Mediterranean and Middle East, which are brined in vinegar or packed in coarse salt to preserve. Best rinsed before using, capers are often used in French, Italian and Greek dishes.

Passion Fruit
Hurricanes

PARTY
DRINKS

PASSION FRUIT HURRICANES

Our version of the famous New Orleans beverage uses real fruit juice. As tropical as a hurricane with just as much punch, this is the perfect summer sipper.

—TASTE OF HOME TEST KITCHEN

START TO FINISH: 10 MIN.
MAKES: 6 SERVINGS

- 2 **cups passion fruit juice**
- 1 **cup plus 2 tablespoons sugar**
- ¾ **cup lime juice**
- ¾ **cup light rum**
- ¾ **cup dark rum**
- 3 **tablespoons grenadine syrup**
- 6 **to 8 cups ice cubes**
  Orange slices, starfruit slices and maraschino cherries

EACH SERVING
- 1 **cup cold water**
  Ice cubes
  Citrus slices, optional
  Mint sprigs, optional

1. In a pitcher, combine the fruit juice, sugar, lime juice, rum and grenadine; stir until sugar is dissolved.

2. Pour into hurricane or highball glasses filled with ice. Serve with orange slices, starfruit slices and cherries.

SWEET TEA CONCENTRATE

This refreshingly sweet cooler is a Southern classic. Whip up a batch to serve at your next party or picnic or make a single glass to sip slowly on a hot, sticky day.

—NATALIE BREMSON PLANTATION, FL

PREP: 30 MIN. + COOLING
MAKES: 20 SERVINGS
(5 CUPS CONCENTRATE)

- 2 **medium lemons**
- 4 **cups sugar**
- 4 **cups water**
- 1½ **cups English breakfast tea leaves or 20 black tea bags**
- ⅓ **cup lemon juice**

1. Remove peels from lemons; set fruit aside for garnish or save for another use.

2. In a large saucepan, combine sugar and water. Bring to a boil over medium heat. Reduce heat; simmer, uncovered, for 3-5 minutes or until sugar is dissolved, stirring occasionally. Remove from the heat; add tea leaves and lemon peels. Cover and steep for 15 minutes. Strain tea, discarding tea leaves and lemon peels; stir in lemon juice. Cool to room temperature.

3. Transfer to a container with a tight-fitting lid. Store in the refrigerator for up to 2 weeks.

TO PREPARE TEA *In a tall glass, combine water with ¼ cup concentrate; add ice. Add citrus slices and mint sprigs if desired.*

QUICK BITES

WHITE SANGRIA

START TO FINISH: 15 MIN. • **MAKES:** 6 SERVINGS

- ¼ **cup sugar**
- ¼ **cup brandy**
- 1 **cup sliced peeled fresh peaches or frozen sliced peaches, thawed**
- 1 **cup sliced fresh strawberries or frozen sliced strawberries, thawed**
- 1 **medium lemon, sliced**
- 1 **medium lime, sliced**
- 3 **cups dry white wine, chilled**
- 1 **can (12 ounces) lemon-lime soda, chilled**
  Ice cubes

In a pitcher, mix sugar and brandy until sugar is dissolved. Add remaining ingredients; stir gently to combine. Serve over ice.

Using white wine instead of red makes my version of sangria a bit lighter, yet with the same wonderful sweetness. Frozen fruit allows me to serve this refreshing sipper any time of year.
—**SHARON TIPTON** CASSELBERRY, FL

White Sangria

ALL-OCCASION PUNCH

Whenever I serve punch, I make it extra fun by adding an ice ring made out of cherry soda. Not only does it keep the punch cold, it adds extra color, too.

—**CAROL VAN SICKLE** VERSAILLES, KY

START TO FINISH: 15 MIN.
MAKES: 22 SERVINGS (1 CUP EACH)

- **8 cups cold water**
- **1 can (12 ounces) frozen lemonade concentrate, thawed plus ¾ cup thawed lemonade concentrate**
- **2 liters ginger ale, chilled**
- **1 liter cherry lemon-lime soda, chilled**
  Ice ring, optional

In a large punch bowl, combine water and lemonade concentrate. Stir in ginger ale and lemon-lime soda. Top with an ice ring if desired. Serve punch immediately.

SPARKLING PEACH BELLINIS

Your guests will love the subtle peach flavor in this elegant champagne.

—TASTE OF HOME TEST KITCHEN

PREP: 35 MIN. + COOLING
MAKES: 12 SERVINGS

- **3 medium peaches, halved**
- **1 tablespoon honey**
- **1 can (11.3 ounces) peach nectar, chilled**
- **2 bottles (750 milliliters each) champagne or sparkling grape juice, chilled**

1. Line a baking sheet with a large piece of heavy-duty foil (about 18 x 12 in.). Place peach halves, cut sides up, on foil; drizzle with honey. Fold foil over peaches and seal.

2. Bake at 375° for 25-30 minutes or until tender. Cool completely; remove and discard peels. In a food processor, process peaches until smooth.

3. Transfer peach puree to a pitcher. Add the nectar and 1 bottle of champagne; stir until combined. Pour into 12 champagne flutes or wine glasses; top with remaining champagne. Serve immediately.

PUNCH POINTERS

Chill all punch ingredients before mixing so that you don't have to dilute the punch with ice to get it cold. Or consider garnishing a cold punch with an ice ring (which lasts longer than ice cubes) made from punch ingredients instead of water.

FROZEN STRAWBERRY DAIQUIRIS

Blend this refreshing ruby-red drink to serve on a hot summer day, at a barbecue or during a Mexican-themed party.

—TASTE OF HOME TEST KITCHEN

START TO FINISH: 10 MIN.
MAKES: 4 SERVINGS

- **¾ cup rum**
- **½ cup thawed limeade concentrate**
- **1 package (10 ounces) frozen sweetened sliced strawberries**
- **1 to 1½ cups ice cubes**
- **GARNISH**
  Fresh strawberries

1. In a blender, combine the rum, limeade concentrate, strawberries and ice. Cover and process until smooth and thickened (use more ice for thicker daiquiris). Pour into cocktail glasses.

2. To garnish each daiquiri, cut a ½-in. slit into the tip of a strawberry; position berry on rim of glass.

PUMPKIN PIE SHOTS

PREP: 25 MIN. + CHILLNG
MAKES: 12 SERVINGS

- 1 **envelope unflavored gelatin**
- 1 **cup cold water**
- ⅓ **cup canned pumpkin**
- ¼ **cup sugar**
- ½ **teaspoon pumpkin pie spice**
- ⅓ **cup butterscotch schnapps liqueur**
- ¼ **cup vodka**
- 1½ **teaspoons heavy whipping cream**
  Sweetened whipped cream

1. In a small saucepan, sprinkle gelatin over cold water; let stand 1 minute. Heat and stir over low heat until gelatin is completely dissolved. Stir in pumpkin, sugar and pie spice; cook and stir until sugar is dissolved. Remove from heat. Stir in liqueur, vodka and cream.

2. Pour mixture into twelve 2-oz. shot glasses; refrigerate until set. Top with sweetened whipped cream.

Set out a batch of these grown-up treats and get ready for the compliments. They can be made ahead of time, making them a great party starter.
—*TASTE OF HOME* TEST KITCHEN

Pumpkin Pie Shots

BANANA NOG

Amaze your friends with this delicious, offbeat take on old-fashioned eggnog. It's well worth the work, and you can make it in advance. Serve the nog with cookies, biscotti and chocolates. Dessert is done!

—JENNAE LEFEBVRE AURORA, IL

PREP: 20 MIN. + CHILLING
MAKES: 11 SERVINGS (ABOUT 2 QUARTS)

- **3 cups milk, divided**
- **3 cups half-and-half cream, divided**
- **3 egg yolks**
- **¾ cup sugar**
- **3 large ripe bananas**
- **½ cup light rum**
- **⅓ cup creme de cacao**
- **1½ teaspoons vanilla extract**
  Whipped cream and baking cocoa, optional

1. In a large heavy saucepan, combine 1½ cups milk, 1½ cups cream, egg yolks and sugar. Cook and stir over medium-low heat until mixture reaches 160° and is thick enough to coat the back of a metal spoon.

2. Place bananas in a food processor; cover and process until blended. Pour milk mixture into a pitcher; stir in the banana puree, rum, creme de cacao, vanilla, and remaining milk and cream. Cover and refrigerate for at least 3 hours before serving.

3. Pour into chilled glasses. Garnish with whipped cream and sprinkle with cocoa if desired.

CHEAT IT! *Substitute 6 cups of eggnog from the dairy case for the milk mixture prepared in the recipe. Stir the banana puree, rum, creme de cacao and vanilla into the eggnog. Garnish as desired.*

MEXICAN HOT CHOCOLATE

START TO FINISH: 15 MIN.
MAKES: 6 SERVINGS

- 4 **cups fat-free milk**
- 3 **cinnamon sticks (3 inches)**
- 5 **ounces 53% cacao dark baking chocolate, coarsely chopped**
- 1 **teaspoon vanilla extract**
  Additional cinnamon sticks, optional

1. In a large saucepan, heat milk and cinnamon sticks over medium heat until bubbles form around sides of pan. Discard cinnamon. Whisk in chocolate until smooth.
2. Remove from the heat; stir in vanilla. Serve in mugs with additional cinnamon sticks if desired.

> The entire family will enjoy this festive drink. Cinnamon sticks give it a great flavor that can't be beat.
> —**PATRICIA NIEH** PORTOLA VALLEY, CA

CREAMSICLE MIMOSAS

Long live childhood! Make a toast to your early years with this "grown up" creamsicle delight. For the kids, mix up a non-alcoholic version using sparkling grape juice, cider or ginger ale.
—**DEIRDRE COX** KANSAS CITY, MO

PREP: 10 MIN. + FREEZING
MAKES: 16 SERVINGS (4 CUPS MIX)

- 2½ **cups orange juice**
- 1 **cup half-and-half cream**
- ¾ **cup superfine sugar**
- 4 **teaspoons grated orange peel**
- 2 **bottles (750 milliliters each) champagne or other sparkling wine**
  Fresh strawberries

1. Place the orange juice, cream, sugar and orange peel in a blender; cover and process until sugar is dissolved. Transfer to an 8-in. square dish. Freeze for 6 hours or overnight.
2. For each serving, scoop ¼ cup mix into a champagne glass; top with Champagne. Garnish with a strawberry and serve immediately.

Sparkling
Cranberry Kiss

SPARKLING CRANBERRY KISS

I love the tartness of cranberries in cold beverages, so this recipe is a keeper. It can be doubled, tripled or even quadrupled.

—SHANNON ARTHUR WHEELERSBURG, OH

START TO FINISH: 5 MIN.
MAKES: 14 SERVINGS (¾ CUP EACH)

- **6 cups cranberry juice**
- **1½ cups orange juice**
- **3 cups ginger ale**
  Ice cubes
  Orange slices, optional

In a pitcher, combine cranberry juice and orange juice. Just before serving, stir in ginger ale; serve over ice. If desired, serve with orange slices.

TEXAS TEA

Make a pitcher full of this beverage for a get-together on a hot summer day. It's a potent drink, so limit yourself to one or two.

—*TASTE OF HOME* TEST KITCHEN

START TO FINISH: 10 MIN.
MAKES: 8 SERVINGS

- **1 cup cola**
- **1 cup sour mix**
- **½ cup vodka**
- **½ cup gin**
- **½ cup Triple Sec**
- **½ cup golden or light rum**
- **½ cup tequila**
  Lemon or lime slices

In a pitcher, combine the first seven ingredients; serve over ice. Garnish servings with lemon.

SPICED COFFEE

Even people who don't usually drink coffee will find this special chocolaty blend that's simmered in the slow cooker appealing.

—JOANNE HOLT BOWLING GREEN, OH

PREP: 10 MIN. • **COOK:** 2 HOURS
MAKES: 8 SERVINGS

- 8 **cups brewed coffee**
- ⅓ **cup sugar**
- ¼ **cup chocolate syrup**
- ½ **teaspoon anise extract**
- 4 **cinnamon sticks (3 inches)**
- 1½ **teaspoons whole cloves**
  Additional cinnamon sticks, optional

1. In a 3-qt. slow cooker, combine coffee, sugar, chocolate syrup and extract. Place cinnamon sticks and cloves on a double thickness of cheesecloth. Gather corners of cloth to enclose spices; tie securely with string. Add to slow cooker. Cook, covered, on low 2-3 hours.

2. Discard spice bag. If desired, serve coffee with cinnamon sticks.

□□□□□□□□□□□□□□□□□□□□
Ginger-Grapefruit
Fizz
□□□□□□□□□□□□□□□□□□□□

GINGER-GRAPEFRUIT FIZZ

Sometimes it's hard to find a special, non-alcoholic beverage for parties that doesn't fall into the punch category. That's why I love this bubbly drink. It has a little tartness from grapefruit and spice from ginger.
—DAWN VIOLA CLERMONT, FL

PREP: 25 MIN. + CHILLING • **MAKES:** 8 SERVINGS

- **1 cup sugar**
- **1 cup water**
- **½ cup sliced fresh gingerroot**
- **½ teaspoon whole peppercorns**
- **¼ teaspoon vanilla extract**
- **⅛ teaspoon salt**
- **¼ cup coarse sugar**
- **3 cups fresh grapefruit juice, chilled**
  Ice cubes
- **4 cups sparkling water, chilled**

1. In a small saucepan, bring the first six ingredients to a boil. Reduce heat; simmer 10 minutes. Refrigerate until cold. Strain syrup, discarding ginger and peppercorns.

2. Using water, moisten rims of eight cocktail glasses. Sprinkle coarse sugar on a plate; hold each glass upside down and dip rims into sugar. Discard remaining sugar on plate.

3. In a pitcher, combine grapefruit juice and syrup. Pour ½ cup into prepared glasses over ice; top with ½ cup sparkling water.

GINGERROOT 101

Fresh gingerroot is available in your grocer's produce section. It should have a smooth skin. If wrinkled and cracked, the root is dry and past its prime. When stored in a heavy-duty resealable plastic bag, unpeeled gingerroot can be frozen for up to 1 year.

QUICK BITES

COQUITO

An all-time family favorite, this creamy, frozen adult beverage features cream of coconut blended with cloves, cinnamon, vanilla and rum.

—EVELYN ROBLES OAK CREEK, WI

PREP: 15 MIN. + CHILLING
MAKES: 8 SERVINGS

- 1 **can (15 ounces) cream of coconut**
- 1 **can (14 ounces) sweetened condensed milk**
- 1 **can (12 ounces) evaporated milk**
- ½ **cup water**
- 1 **teaspoon vanilla extract**
- ½ **teaspoon ground cinnamon**
- ¼ **teaspoon ground cloves**
- 1 **cup rum**

Place the first seven ingredients in a blender; cover and process until blended. Refrigerate until chilled. Stir in rum before serving.

> There's no last-minute rush when you slowly simmer this punch.
> **—ALPHA WILSON** ROSWELL, NM

SLOW COOKER CIDER

PREP: 5 MIN. • **COOK:** 2 HOURS
MAKES: 2 QUARTS

- 2 **cinnamon sticks (3 inches)**
- 1 **teaspoon whole cloves**
- 1 **teaspoon whole allspice**
- 2 **quarts apple cider**
- ½ **cup packed brown sugar**
- 1 **orange, sliced**

1. Place cinnamon, cloves and allspice in a double thickness of cheesecloth; bring up corners of cloth and tie with a string to form a bag.
2. Place cider and brown sugar in a 3-qt. slow cooker; stir until sugar dissolves. Add spice bag. Place orange slices on top. Cover and cook on low for 2-3 hours or until heated through. Discard spice bag.

QUICK BITES

Slow Cooker Cider

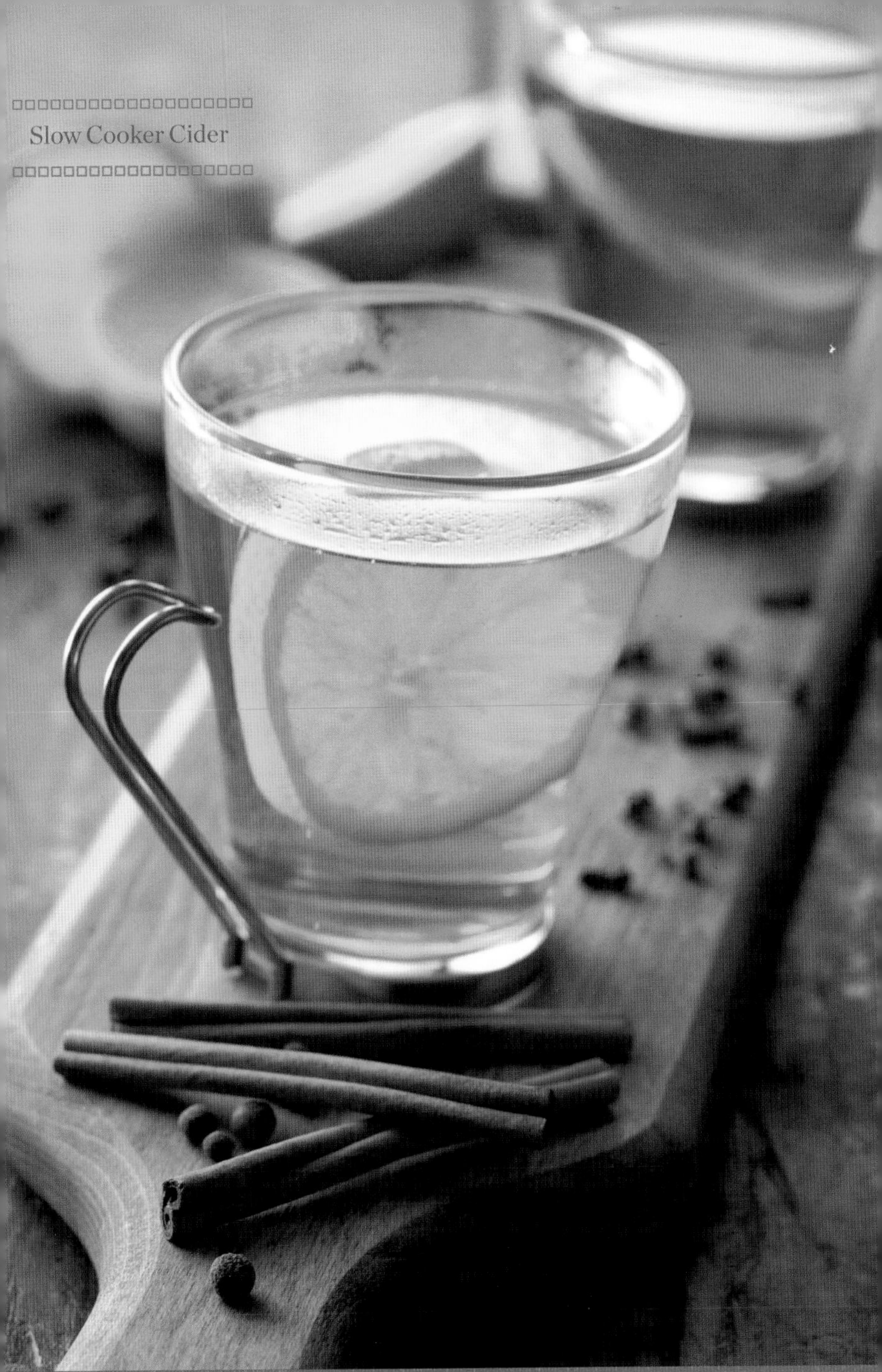

Chai Tea Mix

CHAI TEA MIX

My sister-in-law mixed up this drink for a family gathering. I asked her for the recipe and have been enjoying its warm, spicy flavor ever since.

—DEE FALK STROMSBURG, NE

START TO FINISH: 15 MIN.
MAKES: ABOUT 5 CUPS MIX (26 SERVINGS)

- 3 **cups nonfat dry milk powder**
- 1½ **cups sugar**
- 1 **cup unsweetened instant tea**
- ¾ **cup vanilla powdered nondairy creamer**
- 1½ **teaspoons ground ginger**
- 1½ **teaspoons ground cinnamon**
- ½ **teaspoon ground cardamom**
- ½ **teaspoon ground cloves**

OPTIONAL GARNISH
   Whipped cream

In a food processor, combine all dry ingredients; cover and process until powdery. Store in an airtight container in a cool dry place for up to 6 months.
TO PREPARE 1 SERVING *Dissolve 3 tablespoons of mix in ¾ cup boiling water; stir well. Dollop with whipped cream if desired.*

> ## WHAT IS CHAI?
>
> Chai is the word for tea in many cultures. The hot beverage we think of as chai originated in India. It generally consists of black tea, milk, a sweetener and a blend of seasonings, including cardamom, cinnamon, ginger and cloves.

CERVEZA MARGARITAS

One sip of this refreshing drink and you'll picture sand, sea and blue skies that stretch for miles. It's like a vacation in a glass, and you can mix it up in moments. What are you waiting for?

—CHRISTINA BREMSON PARKVILLE, MO

START TO FINISH: 10 MIN.
MAKES: 5 SERVINGS

   Lime slices and kosher salt, optional
- 1 **can (12 ounces) lemon-lime soda, chilled**
- 1 **bottle (12 ounces) beer**
- 1 **can (12 ounces) frozen limeade concentrate, thawed**
- ¾ **cup tequila**
   Crushed ice

1. If desired, use lime slices to moisten the rims of five margarita or cocktail glasses. Sprinkle salt on a plate; dip rims in salt. Set glasses aside.
2. In a pitcher, combine the soda, beer, limeade concentrate and tequila. Serve in prepared glasses over crushed ice.

BOURBON SLUSH

PREP: 10 MIN. + FREEZING
MAKES: 24 SERVINGS (1 CUP EACH)

- 7 **cups water**
- 1½ **cups sugar**
- 1 **can (12 ounces) frozen orange juice concentrate**
- 1 **can (12 ounces) frozen lemonade concentrate**
- 2 **cups strong brewed tea, cooled**
- 2 **cups bourbon**
- 3 **liters lemon-lime soda, chilled**

1. In a Dutch oven, combine water and sugar; bring to a boil, stirring to dissolve sugar. Remove from heat.
2. Stir in orange juice and lemonade concentrates, tea and bourbon. Transfer to freezer containers; freeze 12 hours or overnight.
3. To serve, place about ½ cup bourbon mixture in each glass; top with ½ cup soda.

> At our holiday parties, Bourbon Slush is definitely a favorite. Have fun experimenting with different teas when you make it. We like black tea, green tea and orange spice.
> —**DARCENE SIGLER** LOUISVILLE, OH

Bourbon Slush

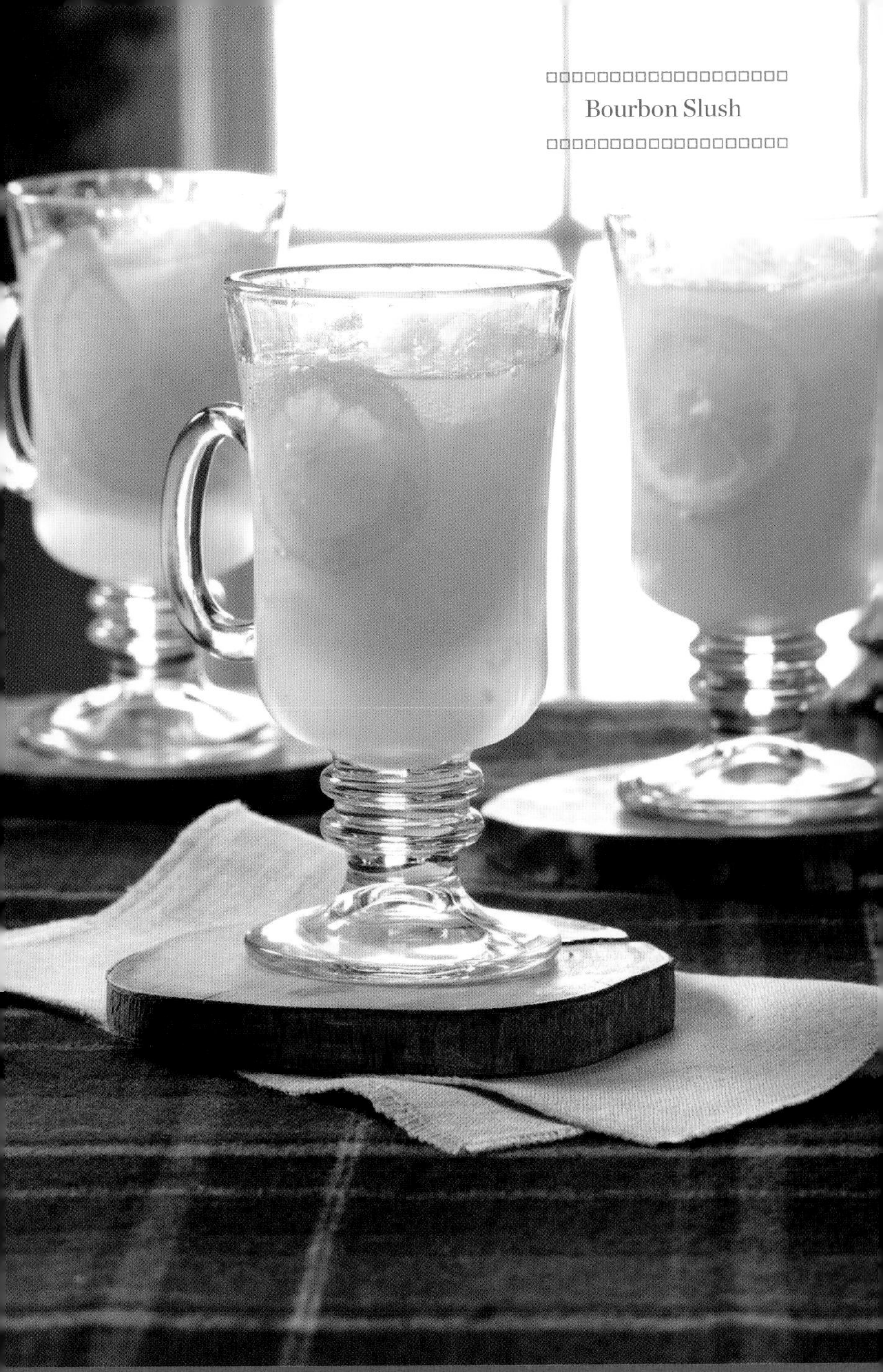

TOPSY-TURVY SANGRIA

I got this recipe from a friend a few years ago. It's perfect for relaxed get-togethers. It tastes best when you make it the night before and let the flavors steep. But be careful—it goes down easy!
—**TRACY FIELD** BREMERTON, WA

START TO FINISH: 10 MIN.
MAKES: 10 SERVINGS (¾ CUP EACH)

- 1 **bottle (750 milliliters) merlot**
- 1 **cup sugar**
- 1 **cup orange liqueur**
- ½ **to 1 cup brandy**
- 3 **cups lemon-lime soda, chilled**
- 1 **cup sliced fresh strawberries**
- 1 **medium lemon, sliced**
- 1 **medium orange, sliced**
- 1 **medium peach, sliced**
  Ice cubes

In a pitcher, stir the wine, sugar, orange liqueur and brandy until sugar is dissolved. Stir in soda and fruit. Serve over ice.

Topsy-Turvy Sangria

MULLED WINE

Heat this classic beverage before company arrives. Because once they take in the aroma, they won't be able to wait to try it.

—LANA GRYGA GLEN FLORA, WI

PREP: 5 MIN. • **COOK:** 30 MIN.
MAKES: 6 SERVINGS

- 1 **bottle (750 ml) ruby port**
- 1 **bottle (750 ml) merlot**
- ½ **cup sugar**
- 4 **orange peel strips (1 to 3 inches)**
- 2 **cinnamon sticks (3 inches)**
- 8 **whole allspice**
- 6 **whole cloves**

In a large saucepan, combine all ingredients; bring just to a simmer (do not boil). Reduce heat; simmer gently, uncovered, 30 minutes or until flavors are blended, stirring to dissolve sugar. Strain. Serve warm.

AUNT FRANCES' LEMONADE

My sister and I spent a week each summer with our Aunt Frances, who always had this thirst-quenching lemonade in a stoneware crock in the refrigerator. It makes a cool and refreshing drink after a hot day soaking up fresh air and sunshine.

—DEBBIE REINHART NEW CUMBERLAND, PA

START TO FINISH: 15 MIN.
MAKES: 12-16 SERVINGS (1 GALLON)

- **5 lemons**
- **5 limes**
- **5 oranges**
- **3 quarts water**
- **1½ to 2 cups sugar**

1. Squeeze the juice from four of the lemons, limes and oranges; pour into a gallon container.

2. Thinly slice the remaining fruit and set aside for garnish. Add water and sugar; mix well. Store in the refrigerator. Serve lemonade over ice with fruit slices.

> There's nothing I love more than coming in from the cold during the winter and smelling the aroma of this heartwarming cider simmering in the slow cooker.
>
> —**MARLENE WICZEK** LITTLE FALLS, MN

HOT SPICED CHERRY CIDER

PREP: 5 MIN. • **COOK:** 4 HOURS
MAKES: 4 QUARTS

- 1 gallon apple cider or juice
- 2 cinnamon sticks (3 inches)
- 2 packages (3 ounces each) cherry gelatin

Place cider in a 6-qt. slow cooker; add cinnamon sticks. Cover and cook on high for 3 hours. Stir in gelatin; cook 1 hour longer. Discard cinnamon sticks before serving.

BUTTERSCOTCH MARTINIS

For guests who want to sip a little something sweet, we dress up our vodka martinis with butterscotch schnapps and chocolate.

—**CLARA COULSON MINNEY**
WASHINGTON COURT HOUSE, OH

START TO FINISH: 10 MIN.
MAKES: 2 SERVINGS

- Ice cubes
- 2 ounces clear creme de cacao
- 2 ounces creme de cacao
- 1½ ounces vodka
- 1½ ounces butterscotch schnapps liqueur
- 6 semisweet chocolate chips

1. Fill a shaker three-fourths full with ice. Add the creme de cacao, vodka and schnapps.
2. Cover and shake for 10-15 seconds or until condensation forms on outside of shaker. Divide chocolate chips between two chilled cocktail glasses; strain butterscotch mixture over chips.

Meat Lovers'
Snack Mix

SNACKS FOR THE
MANCAVE

MEAT LOVERS' SNACK MIX

I admit, this crunchy appetizer might skew toward the dudes. But everyone will go wild for it on game day. My husband loves that it features all of his favorite foods: salted meats, salted nuts and hot sauce.

—GINA MYHILL-JONES 100 MILE HOUSE, BC

PREP: 15 MIN. • **BAKE:** 50 MIN. + COOLING
MAKES: 6 CUPS

- 1¼ cups wasabi-coated green peas
- ¾ cup salted peanuts
- 3 pepperoni-flavored meat snack sticks (1½ ounces each), cut into bite-size pieces
- 2 ounces beef jerky, cut into bite-size pieces
- ½ cup corn nuts
- ½ cup Rice Chex
- ½ cup Multi Grain Cheerios
- ½ cup crunchy cheese puff snacks
- 2 tablespoons chopped sun-dried tomatoes (not packed in oil)
- ⅓ cup canola oil
- 1½ teaspoons chili powder
- 1½ teaspoons onion powder
- ½ teaspoon hot pepper sauce
- ½ teaspoon soy sauce
- ¼ teaspoon seasoned salt

1. Preheat oven to 250°. Combine first nine ingredients in a large bowl. In a small bowl, whisk oil, chili powder, onion powder, pepper sauce, soy sauce and seasoned salt. Drizzle over cereal mixture and toss to coat.
2. Spread into a greased 15x10x1-in. baking pan. Bake 50 minutes, stirring every 10 minutes. Cool completely on a wire rack. Store in an airtight container.

TACO JOE DIP

My daughter was the first to try this recipe. She thought it was so good she passed it on to me. My husband and I think it's terrific. Because it's made in a slow cooker, it's great for parties or busy days.

—LANG SECREST SIERRA VISTA, AZ

PREP: 5 MIN. • **COOK:** 5 HOURS
MAKES: ABOUT 7 CUPS

- 1 can (16 ounces) kidney beans, rinsed and drained
- 1 can (15¼ ounces) whole kernel corn, drained
- 1 can (15 ounces) black beans, rinsed and drained
- 1 can (14½ ounces) stewed tomatoes, undrained
- 1 can (8 ounces) tomato sauce
- 1 can (4 ounces) chopped green chilies, drained
- 1 envelope taco seasoning
- ½ cup chopped onion
  Tortilla chips

In a 5-qt. slow cooker, combine the first eight ingredients. Cover and cook on low for 5-6 hours. Serve with tortilla chips.
NOTE *To make Taco Joe Soup, add a 29-ounce can of tomato sauce to the slow cooker. It will serve 6-8.*

CHEESE FRIES

I came up with this recipe after my daughter had cheese fries at a restaurant and couldn't stop talking about them. She loves that I can fix them so quickly at home.

—MELISSA TATUM GREENSBORO, NC

START TO FINISH: 20 MIN.
MAKES: 8-10 SERVINGS

- 1 package (28 ounces) frozen steak fries
- 1 can (10¾ ounces) condensed cheddar cheese soup, undiluted
- ¼ cup 2% milk
- ½ teaspoon garlic powder
- ¼ teaspoon onion powder
  Paprika

1. Arrange the steak fries in a single layer in two greased 15x10x1-in. baking pans. Bake at 450° for 15-18 minutes or until tender and golden brown.
2. Meanwhile, in a small saucepan, combine the soup, milk, garlic powder and onion powder; heat through. Drizzle over fries; sprinkle with paprika.

PIZZA LOAF

Because this savory stromboli relies on frozen bread dough, it comes together in no time. The golden loaf is stuffed with cheese, pepperoni, mushrooms, peppers and olives. I often add a few thin slices of ham, too. It's tasty served with warm pizza sauce for dipping.

—JENNY BROWN WEST LAFAYETTE, IN

PREP: 20 MIN. • **BAKE:** 35 MIN.
MAKES: 10-12 SLICES

- 1 loaf (1 pound) frozen bread dough, thawed
- 2 eggs, separated
- 1 tablespoon grated Parmesan cheese
- 1 tablespoon olive oil
- 1 teaspoon minced fresh parsley
- 1 teaspoon dried oregano
- ½ teaspoon garlic powder
- ¼ teaspoon pepper
- 8 ounces sliced pepperoni
- 2 cups (8 ounces) shredded part-skim mozzarella cheese
- 1 can (4 ounces) mushroom stems and pieces, drained
- ¼ to ½ cup pickled pepper rings
- 1 medium green pepper, diced
- 1 can (2¼ ounces) sliced ripe olives
- 1 can (15 ounces) pizza sauce

1. Preheat oven to 350°. On a greased baking sheet, roll out dough into a 15x10-in. rectangle. In a small bowl, combine the egg yolks, Parmesan cheese, oil, parsley, oregano, garlic powder and pepper. Brush over the dough.
2. Sprinkle with the pepperoni, mozzarella cheese, mushrooms, pepper rings, green pepper and olives. Roll up, jelly-roll style, starting with a long side; pinch seam to seal and tuck ends under.
3. Place seam side down; brush with egg whites. Do not let rise. Bake 35-40 minutes or until golden brown. Warm the pizza sauce; serve with sliced loaf.
FREEZE OPTION *Freeze cooled unsliced pizza loaf in heavy-duty foil. To use, remove from freezer 30 minutes before reheating. Remove from foil and reheat loaf on a greased baking sheet in a preheated 325° oven until heated through. Serve as directed.*

Pizza Loaf

FRIED PICKLE COINS

If you've never tried fried pickles, step up to the plate and try these puffy golden bites. They're a delicious accompaniment to a burger or a sandwich. For a fun and different appetizer, serve fried pickle slices with ranch dressing for a dip.

—CHERYL WILT EGLON, WV

START TO FINISH: 25 MIN.
MAKES: 8 SERVINGS

- 2 **cups all-purpose flour**
- ½ **teaspoon salt**
- ¼ **teaspoon pepper**
- 2 **eggs**
- 1 **cup milk**
- 3 **cups thin dill pickle slices, drained**
    Oil for deep-fat frying
    Ranch salad dressing, optional

1. In a shallow bowl, combine the flour salt and pepper. In another bowl, beat eggs and milk. Blot pickles with paper towels to remove moisture. Coat pickle with flour mixture, then dip in egg mixture; coat again with flour mixture.
2. In an electric skillet or deep-fat fryer, heat oil to 375°. Fry pickles, about 10 at a time, for 3 minutes or until golden brown, turning once. Drain on paper towels. Serve warm with ranch dressing if desired.

SOFT BEER PRETZELS

What goes together better than beer and pretzels? Not much that I can think of. That's why I put them together into one delicious recipe. I'm always looking for new ways to combine fun flavors and these pretzels hit the spot.
—ALYSSA WILHITE WHITEHOUSE, TX

PREP: 1 HOUR + RISING • **BAKE:** 10 MIN.
MAKES: 8 PRETZELS

- 1 **bottle (12 ounces) amber beer or nonalcoholic beer**
- 1 **package (¼ ounce) active dry yeast**
- 2 **tablespoons unsalted butter, melted**
- 2 **tablespoons sugar**
- 1½ **teaspoons salt**
- 4 **to 4½ cups all-purpose flour**
- 10 **cups water**
- ⅔ **cup baking soda**

TOPPING
- 1 **egg yolk**
- 1 **tablespoon water**
  Coarse salt

1. In a small saucepan, heat beer to 110°-115°; remove from heat. Stir in yeast until dissolved. In a large bowl, combine butter, sugar, 1½ teaspoons salt, yeast mixture and 3 cups flour; beat on medium speed until smooth. Stir in enough remaining flour to form a soft dough (dough will be sticky).
2. Turn dough onto a floured surface; knead until smooth and elastic, about 6-8 minutes. Place in a greased bowl, turning once to grease the top. Cover with plastic wrap and let rise in a warm place until doubled, about 1 hour.
3. Preheat oven to 425°. Punch dough down. Turn onto a lightly floured surface; divide and shape into eight balls. Roll each into a 24-in. rope. Curve ends of each rope to form a circle; twist ends once and lay over opposite side of circle, pinching ends to seal.
4. In a Dutch oven, bring water and baking soda to a boil. Drop pretzels, two at a time, into boiling water. Cook 30 seconds. Remove with a slotted spoon; drain well on paper towels.
5. Place 2 in. apart on greased baking sheets. In a small bowl, whisk egg yolk and water; brush over pretzels. Sprinkle with coarse salt. Bake 10-12 minutes or until golden brown. Remove from pans to a wire rack to cool.

FREEZE OPTION *Freeze cooled pretzels in resealable plastic freezer bags. To use, thaw at room temperature or, if desired, microwave each pretzel on high 20-30 seconds or until heated through.*

TO MAKE TRADITIONAL-SHAPED PRETZELS: *Divide and shape dough into eight balls; roll each into a 24-in. rope. Curve ends of rope to form a circle; twist ends once and lay over opposite side of circle, pinching ends to seal. Boil, top and bake as directed. Yield: 8 pretzels.*

TO MAKE PRETZEL BITES: *Divide and shape into eight balls; roll each into a 12-in. rope. Cut each rope into 1-in. pieces. Boil and top as directed; bake at 400° for 6-8 minutes or until golden brown. Yield: 8 dozen.*

SPICY SWEET POTATO CHIPS & CILANTRO DIP

This cool, creamy dip is a great partner for spicy sweet potato chips. The flavors complement each other so well I can't imagine eating one without the other.

—LIBBY WALP CHICAGO, IL

PREP: 20 MIN. • **BAKE:** 25 MIN./BATCH
MAKES: 12 SERVINGS (1½ CUPS DIP)

- **2 to 3 large sweet potatoes (1¾ pounds), peeled and cut into ⅛-inch slices**
- **2 tablespoons canola oil**
- **1 teaspoon chili powder**
- **½ teaspoon garlic powder**
- **½ teaspoon taco seasoning**
- **¼ teaspoon salt**
- **¼ teaspoon ground cumin**
- **¼ teaspoon pepper**
- **⅛ teaspoon cayenne pepper**

DIP
- **¾ cup mayonnaise**
- **½ cup sour cream**
- **2 ounces cream cheese, softened**
- **4½ teaspoons minced fresh cilantro**
- **1½ teaspoons lemon juice**
- **½ teaspoon celery salt**
- **⅛ teaspoon pepper**

1. Place sweet potatoes in a large bowl. In a small bowl, mix oil and seasonings; drizzle over potatoes and toss to coat.

2. Arrange potatoes in a single layer in two ungreased 15x10x1-in. baking pans. Bake at 400° for 25-30 minutes or until golden brown, turning once. Repeat with remaining potatoes.

3. In a small bowl, beat dip ingredients until blended. Serve with chips.

Spicy Sweet Potato
Chips & Cilantro Dip

GUACAMOLE APPETIZER SQUARES

This cold appetizer pizza has appeared at family functions for many years. We love it, and I know you'll love it, too.

—**LAURIE PESTER** COLSTRIP, MT

PREP: 20 MIN. • **BAKE:** 10 MIN. + COOLING
MAKES: ABOUT 3 DOZEN

- 2 **tubes (8 ounces each) refrigerated crescent rolls**
- 1½ **teaspoons taco seasoning**
- 1 **package (1 pound) sliced bacon, diced**
- 1 **package (8 ounces) cream cheese, softened**
- 1½ **cups guacamole**
- 3 **plum tomatoes, chopped**
- 1 **can (2¼ ounces) sliced ripe olives, drained**

1. Unroll both tubes of crescent roll dough and pat into an ungreased 15x10x1-in. baking pan; seal seams and perforations. Build up edges. Prick dough with a fork; sprinkle with taco seasoning. Bake at 375° for 10-12 minutes or until golden brown. Cool completely on a wire rack.

2. In a large skillet, cook bacon over medium heat until crisp. Using a slotted spoon, remove to paper towels. In a small bowl, beat cream cheese and guacamole until smooth.

3. Spread cream cheese mixture over crust. Sprinkle with bacon, tomatoes and olives. Refrigerate until serving. Cut into squares.

STEAK TERIYAKI QUESADILLAS

These gently charred quesadillas embody the definition of cheesy deliciousness. The light smoky flavor goes perfectly with sweet pineapple and savory steak.

—LISA HUFF WILTON, CT

PREP: 20 MIN. + MARINATING
GRILL: 15 MIN. • **MAKES:** 18 WEDGES

- ⅓ **cup reduced-sodium soy sauce**
- ⅓ **cup reduced-sodium chicken broth**
- 1 **tablespoon brown sugar**
- 1 **teaspoon minced fresh gingerroot**
- ½ **teaspoon onion powder**
- 1 **garlic clove, minced**
- 1 **beef top sirloin steak (1 inch thick and ¾ pound)**
- ½ **cup finely chopped fresh pineapple**
- ½ **cup finely chopped red onion**
- ½ **cup finely chopped green pepper**
- 2 **cups (8 ounces) shredded part-skim mozzarella cheese**
- 6 **flour tortillas (8 inches)**

1. In a small bowl, combine the first six ingredients; set aside 3 tablespoons for filling. Pour remaining mixture into a large resealable plastic bag. Add the steak; seal bag and turn to coat. Refrigerate for 2 hours.

2. Drain steak and discard marinade. Grill steak, covered, over medium heat or broil 4 in. from the heat for 8-11 minutes on each side or until meat reaches desired doneness (for medium-rare, a meat thermometer should read 145°; medium, 160°; well-done, 170°).

3. Remove steak from the grill and cool slightly; cut into bite-size pieces. In a large bowl, combine the pineapple, red onion, green pepper and beef.

4. Sprinkle half of the cheese over three tortillas. Using a slotted spoon, top with beef mixture. Drizzle with reserved soy mixture. Sprinkle with remaining cheese; top with remaining tortillas.

5. Grill over medium heat for 1-2 minutes on each side or until cheese is melted. Cut each into six wedges; serve immediately.

RANCH SNACK MIX

This is a wonderful fast-to-fix munchie. The recipe makes a generous 24 cups and doesn't involve any cooking. It's a cinch to make for parties or potlucks.

—LINDA MURPHY PULASKI, WI

START TO FINISH: 15 MIN.
MAKES: 6 QUARTS

- 1 **package (12 ounces) miniature pretzels**
- 2 **packages (6 ounces each) Bugles**
- 1 **can (10 ounces) salted cashews**
- 1 **package (6 ounces) miniature cheddar cheese fish-shaped crackers**
- 1 **envelope ranch salad dressing mix**
- ¾ **cup canola oil**

In two large bowls, combine the pretzels, Bugles, cashews and crackers. Sprinkle with dressing mix; toss gently to combine. Drizzle with oil; toss until well coated. Store in airtight containers.

CHICKEN SATAY

These golden skewered chicken snacks are marinated and grilled, then served with a zesty Thai-style peanut butter sauce.

—SUE GRONHOLZ BEAVER DAM, WI

PREP: 15 MIN. + MARINATING • **GRILL:** 5 MIN.
MAKES: 8 SERVINGS (1 CUP SAUCE)

- 2 **pounds boneless skinless chicken breasts**
- ½ **cup 2% milk**
- 6 **garlic cloves, minced**
- 1 **tablespoon brown sugar**
- 1 **tablespoon each ground coriander, ground turmeric and ground cumin**
- 1 **teaspoon salt**
- 1 **teaspoon white pepper**
- ⅛ **teaspoon coconut extract**

PEANUT BUTTER SAUCE

- ⅓ **cup peanut butter**
- ⅓ **cup 2% milk**
- 2 **green onions, chopped**
- 1 **small jalapeno pepper, seeded and finely chopped**
- 2 **to 3 tablespoons lime juice**
- 2 **tablespoons reduced-sodium soy sauce**
- 1 **garlic clove, minced**
- 1 **teaspoon sugar**
- 1 **teaspoon minced fresh cilantro**
- 1 **teaspoon minced fresh gingerroot**
- ⅛ **teaspoon coconut extract**

1. Flatten chicken to ¼-in. thickness; cut lengthwise into 1-in.-wide strips. In a large resealable plastic bag, combine the milk, garlic, brown sugar, seasonings and extract. Add chicken; seal bag and turn to coat. Refrigerate for 8 hours or overnight.

2. In a small bowl, whisk the sauce ingredients until blended. Cover and refrigerate until serving. Drain and discard marinade. Thread two chicken strips onto each metal or soaked wooden skewer.

3. Grill, uncovered, over medium-hot heat for 2-3 minutes on each side or until chicken juices run clear. Serve with peanut butter sauce.

Chicken Satay

LOADED MEXICAN PIZZA

My husband is a picky eater, but this healthy pizza is a dish he actually looks forward to. It has lots of flavor and leftovers are no problem because this is one of those rare foods that tastes better the next day.

—MARY BARKER KNOXVILLE, TN

START TO FINISH: 30 MIN.
MAKES: 6 SLICES

- 1 **can (15 ounces) black beans, rinsed and drained**
- 1 **medium red onion, chopped**
- 1 **small sweet yellow pepper, chopped**
- 3 **teaspoons chili powder**
- ¾ **teaspoon ground cumin**
- 3 **medium tomatoes, chopped**
- 1 **jalapeno pepper, seeded and finely chopped**
- 1 **garlic clove, minced**
- 1 **prebaked 12-inch thin pizza crust**

- 2 **cups chopped fresh spinach**
- 2 **tablespoons minced fresh cilantro**
  Hot pepper sauce to taste
- ½ **cup shredded reduced-fat cheddar cheese**
- ½ **cup shredded pepper Jack cheese**

1. In a small bowl, mash black beans. Stir in the onion, yellow pepper, chili powder and cumin. In another bowl, combine the tomatoes, jalapeno and garlic.

2. Place crust on an ungreased 12-in. pizza pan; spread with bean mixture. Top with tomato mixture and spinach. Sprinkle with cilantro, pepper sauce and cheeses.

3. Bake at 400° for 12-15 minutes or until cheese is melted.

NOTE *Wear disposable gloves when cutting hot peppers; the oils can burn skin. Avoid touching your face.*

BARBECUE BEEF TACO PLATES

prepared this hearty appetizer for 200
people at a cookout, and it was gone before
knew it! Everyone loved the combination
f barbecued ground beef, veggies and
heddar cheese.

–IOLA EGLE BELLA VISTA, AR

REP: 20 MIN. • **COOK:** 20 MIN.
MAKES: 2 PLATES (20 SERVINGS EACH)

- **4 pounds ground beef**
- **2 envelopes taco seasoning**
- **1 cup water**
- **4 packages (8 ounces each) cream cheese, softened**
- **1 cup 2% milk**
- **2 envelopes ranch salad dressing mix**
- **4 cans (4 ounces each) chopped green chilies, drained**
- **1 cup chopped green onions**
- **3 to 4 cups shredded romaine**
- **2 cups (8 ounces) shredded cheddar cheese**
- **4 medium tomatoes, seeded and chopped**
- **2 to 3 cups honey barbecue sauce**
- **2 to 3 packages (13½ ounces each) tortilla chips**

1. In a Dutch oven, cook beef over
medium heat until no longer pink;
drain. Stir in taco seasoning and water.
Bring to a boil. Reduce heat; simmer,
uncovered, for 15 minutes.
2. In a large bowl, beat the cream
cheese, milk and dressing mixes until
blended. Spread over two 14-in. plates.
Layer with the beef mixture, chilies,
onions, romaine, cheese and tomatoes.
Drizzle with barbecue sauce.
3. Arrange some tortilla chips around
the edge; serve with remaining chips.

MEATBALL CALZONES

My family can't get enough of this savory
entree. We have it at least once a month.
Leftovers freeze well for a quick meal later.
—CORI COOPER BOISE, ID

PREP: 1½ HOURS + STANDING
BAKE: 25 MIN.
MAKES: 3 CALZONES (4 SERVINGS EACH)

- **3 eggs, lightly beaten**
- **1 cup seasoned bread crumbs**
- **1 cup grated Parmesan cheese**
- **3 teaspoons Italian seasoning**
- **2 pounds ground beef**
- **3 loaves (1 pound each) frozen bread dough, thawed**
- **3 cups (12 ounces) shredded part-skim mozzarella cheese**
- **1 egg white, lightly beaten**
  Additional Italian seasoning
- **1 jar (14 ounces) spaghetti sauce, warmed**

1. In a large bowl, combine the eggs,
bread crumbs, Parmesan cheese and
Italian seasoning. Crumble beef over
mixture; mix well. Shape into 1-in. balls.
2. Place meatballs on a rack in a
shallow baking pan. Bake, uncovered, at
400° for 10-15 minutes or until no
longer pink. Drain on paper towels.
Reduce heat to 350°.
3. On a floured surface, roll each
portion of dough into an 18x12-in.
rectangle. Spoon a third of the
meatballs and mozzarella cheese down
the center of each rectangle. Fold dough
over filling; press edges firmly to seal.
4. Place on greased baking sheets.
Brush tops with egg white; sprinkle
with Italian seasoning. Let stand for
15-30 minutes. Bake for 25-30 minutes
or until golden brown. Serve with
spaghetti sauce.

MEAT-ATARIAN SUB

This recipe started out as amped-up garlic bread and turned into an unforgettable football day sub sandwich.

—SHANON MAYER EVANSTON, WY

PREP: 20 MIN. • **BAKE:** 25 MIN.
MAKES: 6 SERVINGS

- 1 cup (4 ounces) shredded part-skim mozzarella cheese
- ½ cup grated Parmesan cheese
- ½ cup butter, softened
- ½ cup mayonnaise
- 2 garlic cloves, minced
- 1 teaspoon Italian seasoning
- ¼ teaspoon crushed red pepper flakes
- ¼ teaspoon pepper
- 1 loaf (1 pound) French bread, halved lengthwise
- 1 pound sliced deli ham
- 2 packages (2.1 ounces each) ready-to-serve fully cooked bacon, warmed
- 4 ounces sliced pepperoni
- ½ cup pizza sauce

1. Preheat oven to 350°. In a small bowl, combine first eight ingredients. Spread over cut sides of bread. Layer with ham, bacon, pepperoni and pizza sauce; replace top.

2. Wrap in foil; place on a large baking sheet. Bake 25-30 minutes or until heated through. Cut into slices.

BUFFALO CHICKEN DIP

START TO FINISH: 30 MIN.
MAKES: ABOUT 2 CUPS

- 1 package (8 ounces) cream cheese, softened
- 1 can (10 ounces) chunk white chicken, drained
- ½ cup buffalo wing sauce
- ½ cup ranch salad dressing
- 2 cups (8 ounces) shredded Colby-Monterey Jack cheese
  French bread baguette slices, celery ribs or tortilla chips, optional

1. Preheat oven to 350°. Spread cream cheese into an ungreased shallow 1-qt. baking dish. Layer with chicken, wing sauce and salad dressing. Sprinkle with cheese.

2. Bake, uncovered, 20-25 minutes or until cheese is melted. If desired, serve with baguette slices.

> Buffalo wing sauce, cream cheese and ranch make a great-tasting party dip. Everywhere I take it, people want the recipe.
> **—PEGGY FOSTER** FLORENCE, KY

Buffalo Chicken Dip

HAVARTI SHRIMP QUESADILLAS

Apricot preserves add a touch of sweetness to the mushrooms, shrimp and cheese inside these grilled quesadillas. Or cook them in a hot skillet until lightly browned. Serve them with lime wedges if you'd like.

—SUSAN MANNING BURLINGTON, NC

START TO FINISH: 25 MIN.
MAKES: 2 DOZEN

- ½ **pound fresh mushrooms, chopped**
- 1 **tablespoon canola oil**
- 1 **tablespoon butter**
- 6 **tablespoons apricot preserves**
- 6 **flour tortillas (10 inches)**
- 6 **ounces Havarti cheese, thinly sliced**
- ½ **pound cooked medium shrimp, peeled and deveined and chopped**
- 2 **tablespoons butter, melted**

1. In a large skillet, saute mushrooms in oil and butter until tender. Spread 1 tablespoon preserves over half of each tortilla; top with cheese, shrimp and mushrooms. Fold tortillas over. Brush both sides with melted butter.

2. Grill quesadillas, uncovered, over medium heat for 1-2 minutes on each side or until golden brown and cheese is melted. Cut each quesadilla into four wedges. Serve warm.

SUGARED PEANUTS

I make these yummy peanuts only for special occasions because I cannot keep my husband and son (and myself!) away from them. They never last long, so I recommend making a double batch.

—POLLY HALL ROCKFORD, MI

PREP: 20 MIN. • **BAKE:** 30 MIN. + COOLING
MAKES: 5 CUPS

- 5 **cups unsalted peanuts**
- 1 **cup sugar**
- 1 **cup water**
- ¼ **teaspoon salt**

1. In a large heavy saucepan, combine the peanuts, sugar and water. Bring to a boil; cook until syrup has evaporated, about 10 minutes.
2. Spread peanuts in a single layer in a greased 15x10x1-in. baking pan; sprinkle with salt.
3. Bake at 300° for 30-35 minutes or until dry and lightly browned. Cool completely. Store in an airtight container.

CHILI CONEY DOGS

Everyone in our family, from smallest kids to oldest adults, loves these dogs. They're so easy to throw together and heat in the slow cooker.

—MICHELE HARRIS VICKSBURG, MI

PREP: 20 MIN. • **COOK:** 4 HOURS
MAKES: 8 SERVINGS

- 1 **pound lean ground beef (90% lean)**
- 1 **can (15 ounces) tomato sauce**
- ½ **cup water**
- 2 **tablespoons Worcestershire sauce**
- 1 **tablespoon dried minced onion**
- ½ **teaspoon garlic powder**
- ½ **teaspoon ground mustard**
- ½ **teaspoon chili powder**
- ½ **teaspoon pepper**
  Dash cayenne pepper
- 8 **hot dogs**
- 8 **hot dog buns, split**
  Optional toppings: shredded cheddar cheese, relish and chopped onion

1. In a large skillet, cook beef over medium heat 6-8 minutes or until no longer pink, breaking into crumbles; drain. Stir in tomato sauce, water, Worcestershire sauce, onion and seasonings.
2. Place hot dogs in a 3-qt. slow cooker; top with beef mixture. Cook, covered, on low 4-5 hours or until heated through. Serve on buns with toppings as desired.

KEEP THE LID ON

The lid on your slow cooker seals in steam that cooks the food. So unless the recipe instructs you to stir in or add ingredients, do not lift the lid while the slow cooker is cooking the food.

PHILLY CHEESESTEAK BITES

Here's a deliciously downsized version of the ever-popular Philly cheesesteak. For perfect bite-size snacks, the sandwich ingredients are layered on waffle-cut fries instead of buns.

—*TASTE OF HOME* TEST KITCHEN

PREP: 30 MIN. • **COOK:** 5 MIN.
MAKES: 1½ DOZEN

- 1 **package (22 ounces) frozen waffle-cut fries**
- 1 **medium onion, halved and sliced**
- ½ **small green pepper, halved and sliced**
- ½ **small sweet red pepper, halved and sliced**
- 3 **tablespoons canola oil, divided**
- ½ **teaspoon salt, divided**
- ¾ **pound beef ribeye steak, cut into thin strips**
- ¼ **teaspoon pepper**
- 3 **tablespoons ketchup**
- 6 **tablespoons process cheese sauce**

1. Bake 18 large waffle fries according to package directions (save remaining fries for another use). Meanwhile, in a large skillet, saute onion and peppers in 1 tablespoon oil until tender. Sprinkle with ⅛ teaspoon salt. Remove and keep warm.

2. In the same pan, saute steak in remaining oil in batches for 45-60 seconds or until desired doneness. Sprinkle with pepper and remaining salt. On each waffle fry, layer the beef, onion mixture, ketchup and cheese sauce. Serve warm.

SWEET & SPICY JALAPENO POPPERS

There's no faster way to get a party started than with these bacon-wrapped poppers. Make them ahead of time and bake just before serving.

—DAWN ONUFFER CRESTVIEW, FL

START TO FINISH: 30 MIN.
MAKES: 1 DOZEN

- 6 **jalapeno peppers**
- 4 **ounces cream cheese, softened**
- 2 **tablespoons shredded cheddar cheese**
- 6 **bacon strips, halved widthwise**
- ¼ **cup packed brown sugar**
- 1 **tablespoon chili seasoning mix**

1. Cut jalapenos in half lengthwise and remove seeds; set aside. In a small bowl, beat cheeses until blended. Spoon into pepper halves. Wrap a half-strip of bacon around each pepper half.

2. Combine brown sugar and chili seasoning; coat peppers with sugar mixture. Place in a greased 15x10x1-in. baking pan.

3. Bake at 350° for 18-20 minutes or until bacon is firm.

NOTE *Wear disposable gloves when cutting hot peppers; the oils can burn skin. Avoid touching your face.*

Baked Chicken Nachos

BAKED CHICKEN NACHOS

Here's a colorful party appetizer that's delicious and so simple. Rotisserie (or leftover) chicken keeps it quick, and the seasonings and splash of lime juice lend fantastic flavor. My husband likes this snack so much that he often requests it for dinner!

—GAIL CAWSEY GENESEO, IL

PREP: 20 MIN. • **BAKE:** 15 MIN.
MAKES: 16 SERVINGS

- 2 medium sweet red peppers, diced
- 1 medium green pepper, diced
- 3 teaspoons canola oil, divided
- 1 can (15 ounces) black beans, rinsed and drained
- 1 teaspoon minced garlic
- 1 teaspoon dried oregano
- ¼ teaspoon ground cumin
- 2¼ cups shredded rotisserie chicken
- 4½ teaspoons lime juice
- ⅛ teaspoon salt
- ⅛ teaspoon pepper
- 7½ cups tortilla chips
- 8 ounces pepper Jack cheese, shredded
- ¼ cup thinly sliced green onions
- ½ cup minced fresh cilantro
- 1 cup (8 ounces) sour cream
- 2 to 3 teaspoons diced pickled jalapeno peppers, optional

1. In a large skillet, saute peppers in 1½ teaspoons oil for 3 minutes or until crisp-tender; transfer to a small bowl. In the same skillet, saute the beans, garlic, oregano and cumin in remaining oil for 3 minutes or until heated through.

2. Meanwhile, combine the chicken, lime juice, salt and pepper. In a greased 13x9-in. baking dish, layer half of the tortilla chips, pepper mixture, bean mixture, chicken, cheese, onions and cilantro. Repeat layers.

3. Bake, uncovered, at 350° for 15-20 minutes or until heated through. Serve with sour cream and pickled jalapenos if desired.

QUICK BITES

_____
_____
_____
_____
_____
_____
_____
_____
_____
_____
_____
_____
_____
_____
_____
_____
_____
_____
_____
_____
_____
_____
_____
_____
_____
_____
_____
_____
_____
_____
_____
_____
_____

HOT ARTICHOKE SPINACH DIP

To avoid last-minute fuss, assemble this dip the night before and bake it the next day.
—**CANDY JENSEN** MARRERO, LA

PREP: 20 MIN. • **BAKE:** 30 MIN.
MAKES: 5 CUPS

- ½ cup chopped green onions
- 2 tablespoons butter
- 4 ounces cream cheese, softened
- 2 packages (10 ounces each) frozen creamed spinach, thawed
- 1 can (14 ounces) water-packed artichoke hearts, rinsed, drained and chopped
- 1 cup (4 ounces) shredded Monterey Jack cheese
- 1 cup (4 ounces) shredded Swiss cheese
- 1 tablespoon Worcestershire sauce
- ½ teaspoon Cajun seasoning
- ½ teaspoon minced fresh thyme
- ½ teaspoon hot pepper sauce
- 1 garlic clove, minced
- ¼ cup grated Parmesan cheese
  Toasted baguette slices or pita chips

1. In a small skillet, cook onions in butter until tender; set aside. In a bowl, beat cream cheese until smooth. Stir in the onion mixture, spinach, artichokes, Monterey Jack and Swiss cheeses, Worcestershire sauce, Cajun seasoning, thyme, hot pepper sauce and garlic.

2. Transfer mixture to a greased 1½-qt. baking dish. Bake, uncovered, at 350° for 25-30 minutes or until bubbly around the edges.

3. Top with Parmesan cheese. Broil 4-6 in. from the heat for 3-5 minutes. Serve warm with baguette slices or pita chips. Refrigerate leftovers.

CALZONE PINWHEELS

These pretty bites take advantage of convenient refrigerator crescent rolls and can be made ahead and popped in the oven right before company arrives.
—**LISA SMITH** BRYAN, OH

START TO FINISH: 30 MIN.
MAKES: 16 APPETIZERS

- ½ cup ricotta cheese
- 1 teaspoon Italian seasoning
- ¼ teaspoon salt
- ½ cup shredded part-skim mozzarella cheese
- ½ cup diced pepperoni
- ¼ cup grated Parmesan cheese
- ¼ cup chopped fresh mushrooms
- ¼ cup finely chopped green pepper
- 2 tablespoons finely chopped onion
- 1 package (8 ounces) refrigerated crescent rolls
- 1 jar (14 ounces) pizza sauce, warmed

1. In a small bowl, combine the ricotta cheese, Italian seasoning and salt. Stir in the mozzarella cheese, pepperoni, Parmesan cheese, mushrooms, green pepper and onion. Separate crescent roll dough into four rectangles; seal perforations.

2. Spread cheese mixture over each rectangle to within ¼ in. of edges. Roll up jelly-roll style, starting with a short side; pinch seams to seal. Cut each into four slices.

3. Place cut side down on greased baking sheets. Bake at 375° for 10-15 minutes or until golden brown. Serve warm with pizza sauce. Refrigerate leftovers.

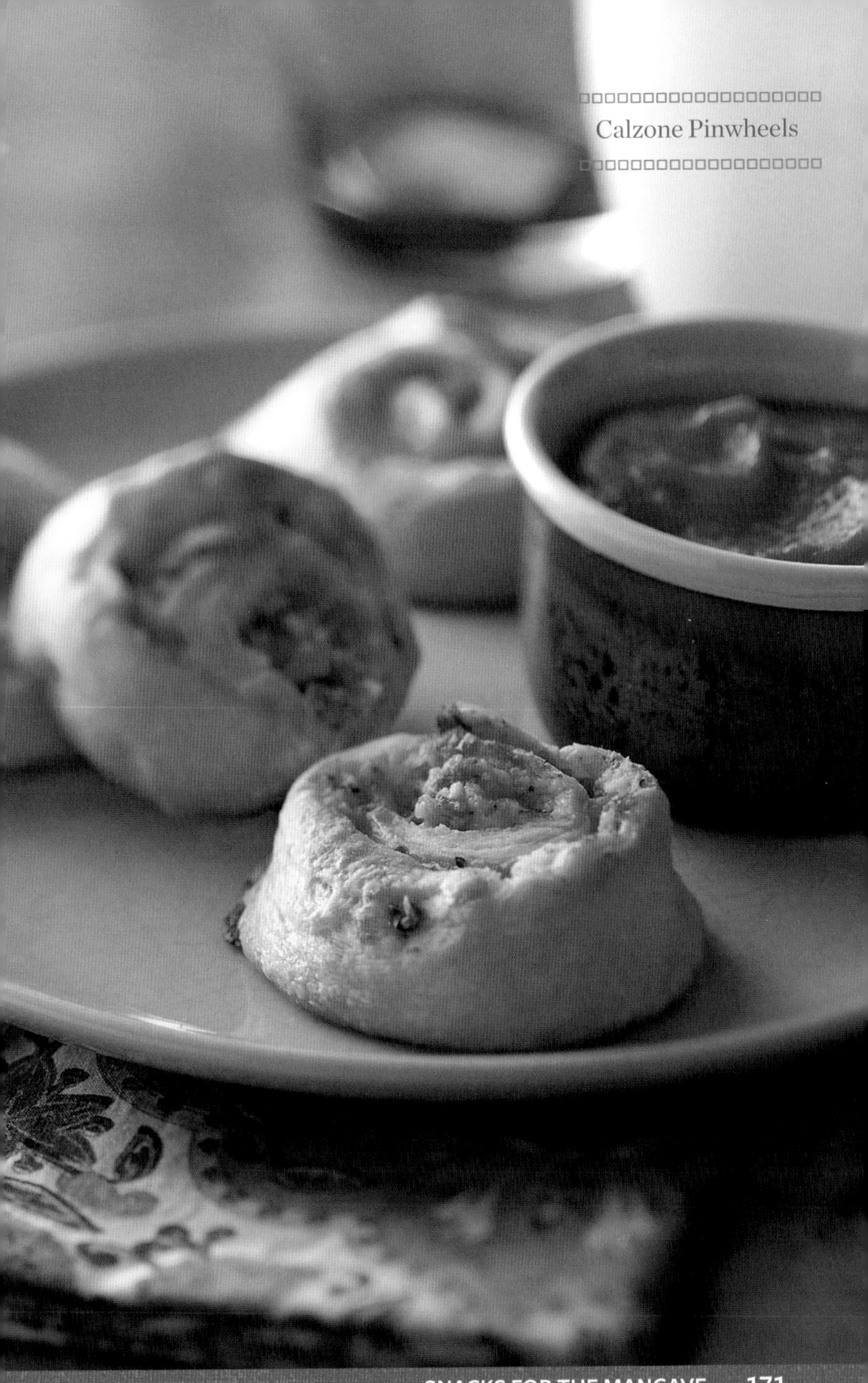

Calzone Pinwheels

SWEET-AND-SOUR CHICKEN WINGS

These wings are a fun appetizer for any gathering, big or small. I also serve them over rice as a main dish. Any way you do it, they'll be a hit!

—JUNE EBERHARDT MARYSVILLE, CA

PREP: 15 MIN. • **COOK:** 3 HOURS
MAKES: 32 APPETIZERS

- 1 **cup sugar**
- 1 **cup cider vinegar**
- ½ **cup ketchup**
- 2 **tablespoons reduced-sodium soy sauce**
- 1 **teaspoon chicken bouillon granules**
- 16 **chicken wings**
- 6 **tablespoons cornstarch**
- ½ **cup cold water**

1. In a small saucepan, combine the first five ingredients. Bring to a boil; cook and stir until sugar is dissolved. Cut wings into three sections; discard wing tip sections.

2. Transfer to a 3-qt. slow cooker; add sugar mixture. Cover and cook on low for 3-4 hours or until chicken juices run clear.

3. Transfer wings to a serving dish and keep warm. Skim fat from cooking juices; transfer to a small saucepan. Bring liquid to a boil.

4. Combine cornstarch and water until smooth. Gradually stir into the pan. Bring to a boil; cook and stir for 2 minutes or until thickened. Spoon over chicken. Serve with a slotted spoon.

NOTE *Uncooked chicken wing sections (wingettes) may be substituted for whole chicken wings.*

COURTSIDE CARAMEL CORN

"I can't stop eating it," my guests tell me when they try my caramel corn. For college basketball game-day parties, I fix enough to fill a big red tin decorated with the University of Arizona logo. The delectable syrup coats the popcorn well but isn't sticky.
—SHARON LANDEEN TUCSON, AZ

PREP: 15 MIN. • **BAKE:** 45 MIN. + COOLING
MAKES: ABOUT 5½ QUARTS

- **6 quarts popped popcorn**
- **2 cups packed brown sugar**
- **1 cup butter, cubed**
- **½ cup corn syrup**
- **1 teaspoon salt**
- **3 teaspoons vanilla extract**
- **½ teaspoon baking soda**

Place popcorn in a large bowl and set aside. In a large saucepan, combine the brown sugar, butter, corn syrup and salt; bring to a boil over medium heat, stirring constantly. Boil for 5 minutes, stirring occasionally.

Remove from the heat. Stir in vanilla and baking soda; mix well. Pour over popcorn and stir until well-coated. Pour into two greased 13x9-in. baking pans.

Bake, uncovered, at 250° for 45 minutes, stirring every 15 minutes. Cool completely. Store in airtight containers.

MARINATED CHEESE WITH PEPPERS AND OLIVES

Cheddar cheese, red peppers and pitted ripe olives make a tasty, rustic appetizer when marinated overnight and served with decorative toothpicks.
—POLLY BRUNNING THAXTON, VA

PREP: 10 MIN. + CHILLING
MAKES: 15 SERVINGS

- **12 ounces cheddar cheese, cut into ¾-inch cubes**
- **2 medium sweet red peppers, cut into ¾-inch pieces**
- **2 cans (6 ounces each) pitted ripe olives, drained**
- **¼ cup canola oil**
- **1 tablespoon white vinegar**
- **1 garlic clove, minced**
- **½ teaspoon dried basil**
- **½ teaspoon dried oregano**

In a large bowl, combine all ingredients. Refrigerate, covered, at least 4 hours or overnight.

QUICK BITES

CRISPY POTATO SKINS

The creamy topping on these is so delicious. They're perfect for snacking on while watching football games.

—**STEPHANIE MOON** BOISE, ID

START TO FINISH: 30 MIN.
MAKES: 4 SERVINGS

- 2 **medium potatoes**
- 1 **tablespoon butter, melted**
- ¼ **cup picante sauce**
- ⅓ **cup shredded cheddar cheese**
- 2 **bacon strips, cooked and crumbled**
- ¼ **cup chopped tomato**
- 2 **tablespoons chopped green onion**

TOPPING

- 3 **tablespoons mayonnaise**
- 2 **tablespoons sour cream**
- 1 **tablespoon prepared ranch salad dressing**
- 1 **bacon strip, cooked and crumbled**
- ¼ **teaspoon garlic powder**

1. Scrub and pierce potatoes. Bake at 400° for 45-50 minutes or until tender. When cool enough to handle, cut each potato lengthwise into four wedges. Cut away the white portion, leaving ¼ in. on the potato skins.

2. Place potato skins on a baking sheet. Brush butter over shells; top with picante sauce, cheese and bacon bits.

3. Bake potatoes, skin side down, at 450° for 12-15 minutes or until cheese is melted and skins are crisp. Sprinkle with tomato and onion. In a small bowl combine topping ingredients. Serve with potato skins.

BEER & CHEDDAR FONDUE

This great-tasting fondue is my mom's favorite, so I make it for her birthday every year. I serve it with apple slices, rye bread cubes and chunks of carrots, mushrooms, celery, zucchini, squash and broccoli.

—**AMANDA WENTZ** VIRGINIA BEACH, VA

START TO FINISH: 15 MIN.
MAKES: 2 CUPS

- 4 **cups (16 ounces) shredded cheddar cheese**
- 1 **tablespoon all-purpose flour**
- 1 **cup beer or nonalcoholic beer**
- 3 **garlic cloves, minced**
- 1½ **teaspoons ground mustard**
- ¼ **teaspoon coarsely ground pepper**
  Pretzel dipping sticks and sliced smoked sausage

1. In a large bowl, combine cheese and flour. In a small saucepan, heat the beer, garlic, mustard and pepper over medium heat until bubbles form around sides of pan.

2. Reduce heat to medium-low; add a handful of cheese mixture. Stir constantly, using a figure-eight motion, until almost completely melted. Continue adding cheese, one handful at a time, allowing cheese to almost completely melt between additions. Keep warm. Serve with pretzels and sausage.

TOUCHDOWN BRAT SLIDERS

It's game time when these minis make an appearance. Two things my husband loves—beer and brats—get stepped up a notch with crunchy flavored chips.

KIRSTEN SHABAZ LAKEVILLE, MN

START TO FINISH: 30 MIN.
MAKES: 16 SLIDERS

- **5 thick-sliced bacon strips, chopped**
- **1 pound uncooked bratwurst links, casings removed**
- **1 large onion, finely chopped**
- **2 garlic cloves, minced**
- **1 package (8 ounces) cream cheese, cubed**
- **1 cup dark beer or nonalcoholic beer**
- **1 tablespoon Dijon mustard**
- **¼ teaspoon pepper**
- **16 dinner rolls, split and toasted**
- **2 cups cheddar and sour cream potato chips, crushed**

1. In a large skillet, cook bacon over medium heat until crisp. Remove to paper towels with a slotted spoon; drain, reserving drippings. Cook bratwurst and onion in drippings over medium heat until meat is no longer pink. Add garlic; cook 1 minute longer. Drain.

2. Stir in the cream cheese, beer, mustard and pepper. Bring to a boil. Reduce heat; simmer, uncovered, for 8-10 minutes or until thickened, stirring occasionally. Stir in bacon. Spoon ¼ cup onto each roll; sprinkle with chips. Replace tops.

Football Fest
Empanadas

FOOTBALL FEST EMPANADAS

Chicken goes well with black beans, corn and jalapenos in these baked Southwestern empanadas.
—JANE WHITTAKER PENSACOLA, FL

PREP: 30 MIN. • **BAKE:** 10 MIN./BATCH
MAKES: 2 DOZEN

- 1 **jar (16 ounces) black bean and corn salsa**
- ½ **cup frozen corn, thawed**
- 2 **jalapeno peppers, seeded and minced**
- 3 **tablespoons minced fresh cilantro, divided**
- 2 **teaspoons lime juice**
- 1 **package (9 ounces) ready-to-use Southwestern chicken strips, chopped**
- 2 **packages (14.1 ounces each) refrigerated pie pastry**
- 4 **ounces quesadilla cheese, shredded**
- 1 **egg, lightly beaten**

- In a large bowl, combine the salsa, corn, jalapenos, 2 tablespoons cilantro and lime juice. In another bowl, combine the chicken, remaining cilantro and ½ cup salsa mixture; set aside. Reserve remaining salsa for serving.
- Unroll a pastry sheet onto a lightly floured surface. Using a floured 4-in. round cookie cutter placed halfway on edge of pastry, cut 4x3-in. football shapes. Repeat with remaining dough, chilling and rerolling scraps as needed.
- Transfer half of the cutouts to greased baking sheets. Place 1 tablespoon chicken mixture in the center of each; top each with 1½ teaspoons cheese. Brush edges of pastry with egg. Top with remaining cutouts; press edges with a fork to seal. Cut slits in the tops to resemble football laces. Brush tops with egg.
- Bake at 450° for 8-12 minutes or until golden brown. Serve warm with reserved salsa mixture. Refrigerate leftovers.

FREEZE OPTION *Freeze cooled pastries in a freezer container, separating layers with waxed paper. To use, reheat pastries on a greased baking sheet in a preheated 400° oven until crisp and heated through.*

QUICK BITES

Gorgonzola Figs
with Balsamic Glaze

HOLIDAYS &
· CELEBRATIONS ·

GORGONZOLA FIGS WITH BALSAMIC GLAZE

PREP: 30 MIN. • **BAKE:** 10 MIN.
MAKES: 16 APPETIZERS

- 1 **cup balsamic vinegar**
- 16 **dried figs**
- ½ **cup crumbled Gorgonzola cheese**
- 8 **thin slices prosciutto, halved widthwise**
- 2 **teaspoons minced fresh rosemary**
- ¼ **teaspoon pepper**

1. For glaze, in a small saucepan, bring vinegar to a boil over medium heat; cook until reduced to about ¼ cup.
2. Cut a lengthwise slit down the center of each fig; fill with 1½ teaspoons cheese. Wrap each with a piece of prosciutto; place on a baking sheet. Sprinkle with rosemary and pepper.
3. Bake at 425° for 10-12 minutes or until the prosciutto is crisp. Serve figs warm with glaze.

NOTE *Amber-colored dried figs (labeled Turkish or Calimyrna) are recommended for this recipe. Mission figs, which are black, are smaller and hold less cheese. If large stems are present, remove them before stuffing figs.*

> For a fancy, eye-catching appetizer, try these delightful stuffed figs wrapped with prosciutto.
> —**SARAH VASQUES** MILFORD, NH

PECANS DIABLO

The spices in this recipe showcase pecans in a brand new light. Enjoy this snack at any party or gathering. We particularly like them in the fall and around Halloween—the heat from the cayenne pepper warms us up on those cool, crisp nights!

—*TASTE OF HOME* TEST KITCHEN

START TO FINISH: 25 MIN.
MAKES: 5 CUPS

- ¼ **cup butter, melted**
- ¾ **teaspoon dried rosemary, crushed**
- ¼ **to ½ teaspoon cayenne pepper**
- ¼ **teaspoon dried basil**
- 5 **cups pecan halves**
- 2 **teaspoons kosher salt**

1. In a large bowl, combine the butter, rosemary, cayenne and basil. Add pecans and toss to coat. Spread in a single layer in a 15x10x1-in. baking pan. Sprinkle with salt.
2. Bake, uncovered, at 325° for 17-20 minutes or until pecans are crisp, stirring occasionally. Cool completely. Store in an airtight container.

SCALLOPS IN SHELLS

My buttery scallops served in a rich, creamy sauce make an excellent first course.

—JANE ROSSEN BINGHAMTON, NY

PREP: 35 MIN. • **BAKE:** 10 MIN.
MAKES: 8 SERVINGS

- 2 **cups water**
- 16 **sea scallops (about 2 pounds)**
- 1 **teaspoon salt**
- 1½ **cups thinly sliced fresh mushrooms**
- 2 **shallots, finely chopped**
- ¼ **cup butter, cubed**

SAUCE

- 2 **tablespoons butter**
- 2 **tablespoons all-purpose flour**
- ¾ **cup 2% milk**
- 2 **tablespoons grated Parmesan cheese**
- 2 **tablespoons sherry**
- ½ **teaspoon salt**
- ¼ **teaspoon lemon juice**
- ¼ **teaspoon pepper**
- ⅛ **teaspoon grated lemon peel**
- 8 **scallop shells**
- ⅓ **cup dry bread crumbs**
- 2 **tablespoons butter, melted**

1. Place water in a large saucepan. Bring to a boil. Reduce heat; add scallops and poach, uncovered, 6 minutes or until firm and opaque. Drain scallops, reserving 1 cup liquid.

2. Sprinkle scallops with salt. In a skillet, saute mushrooms and shallots in butter. Add scallops; cook 2 minutes. Remove from heat; set aside.

3. In a small saucepan, melt butter. Stir in flour until smooth; gradually add milk and reserved liquid. Bring to a boil; cook and stir 2 minutes or until thickened. Stir in cheese, sherry, salt, lemon juice, pepper and lemon peel; add to skillet.

4. Preheat oven to 375°. Divide scallop mixture among eight scallop shells. Combine crumbs and melted butter; sprinkle over tops. Place on an ungreased 15x10x1-in. baking pan. Bake 8-12 minutes or until crumbs are golden brown.

Scallops In Shells

MARGARITA GRANITA WITH SPICY SHRIMP

While tinkering and tuning up recipes for my spring menu, I came up with a snazzy little appetizer that's perfect for Cinco de Mayo. It features two favorites: shrimp and margaritas!

—NANCY BUCHANAN COSTA MESA, CA

PREP: 20 MIN. + FREEZING • **GRILL:** 5 MIN.
MAKES: 8 SERVINGS

- 1 **cup water**
- ½ **cup sugar**
- ½ **cup lime juice**
- 3 **tablespoons tequila**
- 3 **tablespoons Triple Sec**
- 4½ **teaspoons grated lime peel, divided**
- 1 **teaspoon ground cumin**
- 1 **teaspoon smoked paprika**
- 1 **teaspoon ground oregano**
- ½ **teaspoon salt**
- ¼ **teaspoon ground chipotle pepper**
- 16 **uncooked medium shrimp, peeled and deveined**

1. In a large saucepan, bring water and sugar to a boil. Cook and stir until sugar is dissolved. Remove from heat; stir in lime juice, tequila, Triple Sec and 3 teaspoons lime peel.

2. Transfer to an 11x7-in. dish; cool to room temperature. Freeze 1 hour; stir with a fork. Freeze 4-5 hours longer or until completely frozen, stirring every 30 minutes.

3. In a small bowl, combine cumin, paprika, oregano, salt and chipotle pepper; add shrimp, tossing to coat. Thread shrimp onto eight soaked wooden appetizer skewers.

4. Moisten a paper towel with cooking oil; using long-handled tongs, lightly coat grill rack. Grill shrimp, covered, over medium heat or broil 4 in. from heat 3-4 minutes on each side or until shrimp turn pink.

5. Stir granita with a fork just before serving; spoon into small glasses. Top with remaining lime peel; serve with grilled shrimp.

CREOLE SHRIMP & CRAB CHEESECAKE

We live on the beach so seafood is a staple at our house. I love to experiment in the kitchen and came up with this savory dish as a special appetizer.

—CHRISTY HUGHES SUNSET BEACH, NC

PREP: 30 MIN.
BAKE: 1 HOUR + CHILLING
MAKES: 24 SERVINGS

- ¾ cup dry bread crumbs
- ¼ cup grated Parmesan cheese
- ½ teaspoon dill weed
- 2 tablespoons butter, melted

CHEESECAKE

- 2 tablespoons butter
- 1 medium sweet red pepper, finely chopped
- 1 small onion, finely chopped
- 1 medium carrot, finely chopped
- ½ teaspoon dill weed
- ½ teaspoon Creole seasoning
- ¼ teaspoon salt
- ¼ teaspoon pepper
- 3 packages (8 ounces each) cream cheese, softened
- ½ cup heavy whipping cream
- 1 tablespoon sherry or additional cream
- 4 eggs, lightly beaten
- 1 pound peeled and deveined cooked shrimp, chopped
- 2 cans (6 ounces each) lump crabmeat, drained
- 1 cup (4 ounces) shredded Gouda cheese

SAUCE

- 1 cup mayonnaise
- 2 tablespoons Dijon mustard
- ½ teaspoon Creole seasoning
  Assorted crackers

1. Preheat oven to 350°. In a small bowl, mix bread crumbs, Parmesan cheese and dill; stir in butter. Press onto bottom of a greased 9-in. springform pan. Place pan on a baking sheet.

2. For cheesecake, in a large skillet, heat butter over medium-high heat. Add red pepper, onion and carrot; cook and stir until tender. Stir in seasonings. Cool slightly.

3. In a large bowl, beat cream cheese, cream and sherry until smooth. Add eggs; beat on low just until combined. Fold in vegetable mixture, shrimp, crab and Gouda cheese. Pour over crust.

4. Bake 60-65 minutes or until center is almost set. Cool on a wire rack 10 minutes. Loosen sides from pan with a knife. Cool 1 hour longer. Refrigerate overnight, covering when completely cooled.

5. In a small bowl, mix mayonnaise, mustard and Creole seasoning. Remove rim from springform pan. Serve cheesecake with sauce and crackers.

NOTE *The following spices may be substituted for 1 teaspoon Creole seasoning ¼ teaspoon each salt, garlic powder and paprika; and a pinch each of dried thyme, ground cumin and cayenne pepper.*

MARINATED OLIVE & CHEESE RING

We love to make Italian meals into celebrations, and an antipasto always kicks off the party. This one is almost too pretty to eat, especially when sprinkled with pimientos, fresh basil and parsley.

—PATRICIA HARMON BADEN, PA

PREP: 25 MIN. + CHILLING
MAKES: 16 SERVINGS

- 1 package (8 ounces) cold cream cheese
- 1 package (10 ounces) sharp white cheddar cheese, cut into ¼-inch slices
- ⅓ cup pimiento-stuffed olives
- ⅓ cup pitted Greek olives
- ¼ cup balsamic vinegar
- ¼ cup olive oil
- 1 tablespoon minced fresh parsley
- 1 tablespoon minced fresh basil or 1 teaspoon dried basil
- 2 garlic cloves, minced
- 1 jar (2 ounces) pimiento strips, drained and chopped
  Toasted French bread baguette slices

1. Cut cream cheese lengthwise in half; cut each half into ¼-in. slices. On a serving plate, arrange cheeses upright in a ring, alternating cheddar and cream cheese slices. Place olives in center.

2. In a small bowl, whisk vinegar, oil, parsley, basil and garlic until blended; drizzle over cheeses and olives. Sprinkle with pimientos. Refrigerate, covered, at least 8 hours or overnight. Serve with baguette slices.

Marinated Olive
& Cheese Ring

CRAB CAKES WITH RED CHILI MAYO

This has to be one of the most popular appetizers I've made, and it's so attractive for a party. The spicy mayo is just the right accent for the crab cakes.

—TIFFANY ANDERSON-TAYLOR
GULFPORT, FL

PREP: 35 MIN. + CHILLING
COOK: 10 MIN./BATCH
MAKES: 2 DOZEN (1 CUP SAUCE)

- 1⅓ cups mayonnaise
- 2 tablespoons Thai chili sauce
- 2 teaspoons lemon juice, divided
- ¼ cup each finely chopped celery, red onion and sweet red pepper
- 1 jalapeno pepper, seeded and finely chopped
- 4 tablespoons olive oil, divided
- ½ cup soft bread crumbs
- 1 egg, lightly beaten
- 1 pound fresh crabmeat
- ¼ cup all-purpose flour

1. In a small bowl, combine the mayonnaise, chili sauce and 1¼ teaspoons lemon juice. Set aside.

2. In a small skillet, saute the celery, onion, red pepper and jalapeno in 1 tablespoon oil until tender. Transfer to a large bowl; stir in the bread crumbs, egg, ½ cup reserved mayonnaise mixture and remaining lemon juice. Fold in crab. Cover and refrigerate for at least 2 hours. Cover and refrigerate remaining mayonnaise mixture for sauce.

3. Place flour in a shallow bowl. Drop crab mixture by 2 tablespoonfuls into flour. Gently coat and shape into a ½-in.-thick patty. Repeat with remaining mixture.

4. In a large skillet over medium-high heat, cook patties in remaining oil in batches for 3-4 minutes on each side or until golden brown. Serve with reserved sauce.

NOTE *Wear disposable gloves when cutting hot peppers; the oils can burn skin. Avoid touching your face.*

SHRIMP COCKTAIL

Shrimp cocktail was one of the most popular party foods in the 1960s. It's still a crowd favorite. I serve it at all special occasions and at other times as a snack.

—PEGGY ALLEN PASADENA, CA

PREP: 30 MIN. + CHILLING
MAKES: ABOUT 6 DOZEN
(1¼ CUPS SAUCE)

- 3 **quarts water**
- 1 **small onion, sliced**
- ½ **medium lemon, sliced**
- 2 **sprigs fresh parsley**
- 1 **tablespoon salt**
- 5 **whole peppercorns**
- 1 **bay leaf**
- ¼ **teaspoon dried thyme**
- 3 **pounds uncooked large shrimp, peeled and deveined (tails on)**

SAUCE

- 1 **cup chili sauce**
- 2 **tablespoons lemon juice**
- 2 **tablespoons prepared horseradish**
- 4 **teaspoons Worcestershire sauce**
- ½ **teaspoon salt**
  Dash cayenne pepper

1. In a Dutch oven, combine the first eight ingredients; bring to a boil. Add shrimp. Reduce heat; simmer, uncovered, for 4-5 minutes or until shrimp turn pink.

2. Drain shrimp and immediately rinse in cold water. Refrigerate for 2-3 hours or until cold. In a small bowl, combine the sauce ingredients. Refrigerate until serving.

3. Arrange shrimp on a serving platter; serve with sauce.

HOP-TO-IT DEVILED EGGS

Make sweet Easter baskets filled with fantastic flavor. These adorable deviled eggs are a fun project for the kids while the moms and dads finish up preparations for an Easter feast.

—TASTE OF HOME TEST KITCHEN

START TO FINISH: 20 MIN.
MAKES: 1 DOZEN

- 6 **hard-cooked eggs**
- ¼ **cup mayonnaise**
- 1 **tablespoon sweet pickle relish**
- ½ **teaspoon honey mustard**
  Dash salt
  Dash pepper
- ¼ **cup alfalfa sprouts**
- 12 **chives**
- ¼ **cup candy-coated sunflower kernels**

1. Cut eggs in half widthwise. Cut a thin slice from the bottom of each half so they sit flat. Remove yolks; set whites aside. In a small bowl, mash egg yolks. Add the mayonnaise, relish, mustard, salt and pepper; mix well. Stuff or pipe mixture into egg whites.

2. Top with sprouts. Tuck the ends of a chive into each egg, forming a handle. Refrigerate until serving. Just before serving, garnish with sunflower kernels.

BUTTERFLIED SHRIMP ROCKEFELLER

A platter of these light and fresh shrimp bites stands out as a healthy alternative on an appetizer spread.

—**LEE BREMSON** KANSAS CITY, MO

START TO FINISH: 30 MIN.
MAKES: 1½ DOZEN

18 uncooked jumbo shrimp
2 shallots, finely chopped
1 teaspoon dried basil
½ teaspoon fennel seed, crushed
¼ teaspoon pepper
1 tablespoon olive oil
1 garlic clove, minced
1 package (9 ounces) fresh baby spinach, chopped
½ cup dry bread crumbs
1 tablespoon lemon juice
1 tablespoon grated Parmesan cheese

1. Peel and devein shrimp, leaving the tails on. Butterfly each shrimp along the outside curve; set aside.
2. In a large skillet, saute the shallots, basil, fennel seed and pepper in oil until tender. Add garlic; saute for 1 minute. Add spinach; saute 3-4 minutes longer or until wilted. Remove from the heat; stir in bread crumbs and lemon juice.
3. Arrange shrimp on a greased 15x10x1-in. baking pan. Spoon 1 tablespoon spinach mixture over each shrimp; sprinkle with cheese. Bake at 425° for 4-6 minutes or until shrimp turn pink.

HONEY CHAMPAGNE FONDUE

This special fondue has wonderful flavor from champagne, Swiss cheese and honey. It clings well to the fruit and bread dippers.
—**SHANNON ARTHUR** WHEELERSBURG, OH

START TO FINISH: 30 MIN.
MAKES: 3 CUPS

¼ cup finely chopped shallot
1 tablespoon butter
1 garlic clove, minced
1¼ cups champagne
4 teaspoons cornstarch
1 teaspoon ground mustard
¼ teaspoon white pepper
⅓ cup honey
4 cups (16 ounces) shredded Swiss cheese
2 tablespoons lemon juice
Pinch ground nutmeg
French bread cubes, tart apple slices or pear slices

1. In a large saucepan, saute shallot in butter until tender. Add garlic; cook 1 minute longer. Combine the Champagne, cornstarch, mustard and pepper until smooth; gradually stir into pan. Bring to a boil; cook and stir for 2 minutes or until thickened.
2. Stir in honey; heat through. Remove from the heat. Combine cheese and lemon juice; gradually stir into champagne mixture until melted. Keep warm. Sprinkle with nutmeg. Serve with bread cubes, apple or pear slices.

CHICKEN SALAD IN BASKETS

When I first made these cute little chicken cups, they were a big hit. Now my husband often asks me to fix these appetizers for meetings and parties.

—GWENDOLYN FAE TRAPP
STRONGSVILLE, OH

PREP: 15 MIN. • **BAKE:** 15 MIN. + CHILLING
MAKES: 20 APPETIZERS

- 1 cup diced cooked chicken
- 3 bacon strips, cooked and crumbled
- ⅓ cup chopped mushrooms
- 2 tablespoons chopped pecans
- 2 tablespoons diced peeled apple
- ¼ cup mayonnaise
- ⅛ teaspoon salt
  Dash pepper
- 20 slices bread
- 6 tablespoons butter, melted
- 2 tablespoons minced fresh parsley

1. In a small bowl, combine the first five ingredients. Combine the mayonnaise, salt and pepper; add to chicken mixture and stir to coat. Cover and refrigerate until serving.

2. Preheat oven to 350°. Cut each slice of bread with a 3-in. round cookie cutter; brush both sides with butter. Press into ungreased mini muffin cups. Bake 11-13 minutes or until golden brown and crisp.

3. Cool 3 minutes before removing from pans to wire racks to cool completely. Spoon 1 tablespoonful chicken salad into each bread basket. Cover and refrigerate up to 2 hours. Just before serving, sprinkle with parsley.

Tapas Meatballs
with Orange Glaze

PAS MEATBALLS
TH ORANGE GLAZE

p on the outside, moist on the inside, these baked
ese-stuffed meatballs are drizzled with a tasty
et-sour glaze.

ONNIE STALLINGS MARTINSBURG, WV

:P: 25 MIN. • **BAKE:** 20 MIN.
KES: 16 MEATBALLS

- egg, lightly beaten
- cup ketchup
- small onion, finely chopped
- cup soft bread crumbs
- cup minced fresh parsley
- teaspoons paprika
- garlic cloves, minced
- teaspoon salt
- teaspoon pepper
- pound lean ground beef (90% lean)
- ½ ounces feta cheese, cut into sixteen
  ½-in. cubes

AZE

- jar (12 ounces) orange marmalade
- cup orange juice
- green onions, chopped, divided
- jalapeno pepper, seeded and chopped

In a large bowl, combine the first nine
redients. Crumble beef over mixture and mix
l. Divide into 16 portions; flatten. Top each
h a cheese cube; form beef mixture around
ese into meatballs.

Place on a greased rack in a shallow baking
. Bake, uncovered, at 400° for 20-25 minutes
ntil no longer pink. In a small saucepan, heat
marmalade, orange juice, half of the green
ons and the jalapeno.

Place meatballs in a serving dish; pour glaze
r the top and gently stir to coat. Garnish with
naining green onions.

TE *Wear disposable gloves when cutting hot
pers; the oils can burn skin. Avoid touching
r face.*

BEEF WELLINGTON APPETIZERS

Flaky puff pastry, savory beef tenderloin and tangy horseradish cream come together for a delicious holiday-worthy hors d'oeuvre.

—JOAN COOPER SUSSEX, WI

PREP: 45 MIN. • **BAKE:** 15 MIN.
MAKES: 16 APPETIZERS
(1½ CUPS SAUCE)

- 2 **beef tenderloin steaks (8 ounces each), cut into ½-inch cubes**
- 2 **tablespoons olive oil, divided**
- 1¼ **cups chopped fresh mushrooms**
- 2 **shallots, chopped**
- 2 **garlic cloves, minced**
- ⅓ **cup sherry or chicken broth**
- ⅓ **cup heavy whipping cream**
- ½ **teaspoon salt**
- ⅛ **teaspoon pepper**
- 1 **tablespoon minced fresh parsley**
- 1 **package (17.3 ounces) frozen puff pastry, thawed**
- 1 **egg, beaten**

HORSERADISH CREAM
- 1 **cup sour cream**
- ½ **cup mayonnaise**
- 2 **tablespoons prepared horseradish**
- 1 **tablespoon minced chives**
- ¼ **teaspoon pepper**
  Additional minced chives, optional

1. In a large skillet, brown beef in 1 tablespoon oil. Remove and keep wa...

2. In same skillet, saute mushroom... and shallots in remaining oil until tender. Add garlic; cook 1 minute lon... Add sherry, stirring to loosen brown... bits from pan. Stir in cream, salt and pepper. Bring to a boil; cook until liq... is almost evaporated, about 7 minut... Stir in beef and parsley; set aside and keep warm.

3. Preheat oven to 400°. On a lightl... floured surface, unfold puff pastry. R... each sheet into a 12-in. square. Cut e... into 16 squares.

4. Place 2 tablespoonfuls of beef mixture in center of half of squares. ... with remaining squares; press edges... with a fork to seal. Place on parchme... paper-lined baking sheets. Cut slits i... top; brush with egg. Bake 14-16 minu... or until golden brown.

5. In a small bowl, combine horseradish cream ingredients; serv... with appetizers. Garnish with additional chives if desired.

TO MAKE AHEAD *Freeze unbaked pastries on baking sheets until firm, then wrap and store in the freezer for... to 2 months. When ready to use, bak... frozen appetizers at 400° for 16-18 minutes or until golden brown.*

QUICK BITES

Beef Wellington
Appetizers

KIWI TIKI TORCHES

Aloha from Texas! Toasted coconut and macadamia nuts give these simple skewers a Hawaiian flair party-goers will love.

—ELAINE SWEET DALLAS, TX

PREP: 30 MIN. • **COOK:** 10 MIN.
MAKES: 12 SERVINGS

- 1 **fresh pineapple, peeled and cut into 1-inch chunks**
- 4 **medium kiwifruit, peeled and cut into ¾-inch chunks**
- 2 **cups fresh strawberries, halved**

WHITE CHOCOLATE DIPPING SAUCE

- 1 **cup heavy whipping cream**
- 6 **white chocolate Toblerone candy bars (3.52 ounces each), broken into pieces**
- ¼ **cup finely chopped macadamia nuts**
- 1 **to 2 teaspoons rum extract**
- ⅓ **cup flaked coconut, toasted**

1. Alternately thread the pineapple, kiwi and strawberries onto 12 metal o wooden skewers; set aside. In a large saucepan over medium heat, bring cream just to a boil. Reduce heat to lo stir in Toblerone until melted. Remo from the heat; stir in nuts and extract

2. Transfer to a fondue pot and keep warm. Sprinkle with coconut. Serve with fruit kabobs.

NOTE *To toast coconut, bake in a shallow pan in a 350° oven for 5-10 minutes or cook in a skillet over low heat until golden brown, stirring occasionally.*

PUMPKIN CHEESE PUFFS

These fluffy and tender cheese puffs look like mini pumpkins. Romano cheese gives them a nice tang and their cream cheese stems complete the festive look.

TASTE OF HOME TEST KITCHEN

PREP: 20 MIN. • **BAKE:** 20 MIN.
MAKES: 10 SERVINGS

- 2 tablespoons cream cheese, softened
- ½ teaspoon balsamic vinegar
- ½ cup water
- ¼ cup butter, cubed
- ¼ teaspoon salt
- ½ cup all-purpose flour
- 4 drops yellow paste food coloring
- 1 drop red paste food coloring
- ½ cup grated Romano cheese
- 2 eggs
- 10 sprigs fresh Italian parsley, stems removed

1. In a small bowl, combine cream cheese and vinegar. Cover and refrigerate. In a large saucepan, bring the water, butter and salt to a boil. Add flour all at once and stir until a smooth ball forms. Remove from the heat; let stand for 5 minutes.

2. In a small bowl, combine the yellow and red food coloring; stir Romano cheese and food coloring into dough. Add eggs, one at a time; beating well after each addition. Continue beating until mixture is smooth and shiny.

3. Drop by level tablespoonfuls 3 in. apart onto a greased baking sheet. Bake at 400° for 15-20 minutes or until lightly browned. Remove to a wire rack to cool.

4. Using a star tip and reserved cream cheese mixture, pipe stems onto puffs. Add parsley sprigs. Refrigerate leftovers.

DEVILED CRAB

Dip your spoon into this super-rich comfort food, and you might think you're in heaven. Generous portions of crab are mixed with cream and eggs and flavored with chives, onions and more. Mmm!

—DORIS PRILLAMAN WILMINGTON, NC

PREP: 30 MIN. • **BAKE:** 20 MIN.
MAKES: 6 SERVINGS

- ½ cup finely chopped onion
- 3 tablespoons butter
- 3 tablespoons all-purpose flour
- ½ teaspoon salt
- 1½ cups half-and-half cream
- 2 egg yolks, lightly beaten
- 3 cans (6 ounces each) crabmeat, drained, flaked and cartilage removed
- 1 tablespoon Dijon mustard
- 2 teaspoons Worcestershire sauce
- 1 teaspoon minced chives

TOPPING
- 1 cup soft bread crumbs
- 1 tablespoon butter, melted

1. In a large skillet, saute onion in butter until tender. Stir in flour and salt until blended. Gradually stir in cream until smooth. Bring to a boil; cook and stir for 2 minutes or until thickened and bubbly. Remove from the heat.
2. Stir a small amount of hot mixture into egg yolks. Return all to the pan, stirring constantly. Bring to a gentle boil; cook and stir 2 minutes longer. Remove from the heat. Stir in the crab, mustard, Worcestershire sauce and chives.
3. Spoon into six greased 6-oz. ramekins or custard cups. Place on a baking sheet. Combine bread crumbs and melted butter; sprinkle over tops. Bake at 375° for 20-25 minutes or until topping is golden brown.

Deviled Crab

ITALIAN CHEESE WONTONS

A cheesy filling gives wonton wrappers a taste-tempting, Italian twist. The hot and crisp snacks get gobbled up...no matter how many I make!

—**BARBARA PLETZKE** HERNDON, VA

PREP: 25 MIN. + CHILLING
COOK: 5 MIN./BATCH
MAKES: 40 WONTONS

- 2 **cups (8 ounces) shredded Italian cheese blend**
- 1 **carton (15 ounces) ricotta cheese**
- 1 **egg, beaten**
- 1 **tablespoon minced fresh parsley**
- 1 **garlic clove, minced**
- ¼ **teaspoon salt**
- ⅛ **teaspoon pepper**
- 40 **wonton wrappers**
  Oil for deep-fat frying
  Marinara or spaghetti sauce, warmed

1. In a large bowl, combine the first seven ingredients.

2. Position a wonton wrapper with o[ ] point toward you. (Keep remaining wrappers covered with a damp paper towel until ready to use.) Place 1 tablespoon filling in the center of wrapper. Fold bottom corner over filling; fold sides toward center over filling. Roll toward the remaining poi[ ] Moisten top corner with water; press seal. Repeat. Refrigerate for 30 minut[ ]

3. In an electric skillet or deep fryer, heat oil to 375°. Fry wontons, a few at [ ] time, for 1-2 minutes on each side or until golden brown. Drain on paper towels. Serve with marinara.

TO MAKE AHEAD *Prepare the wonton filling the day before. Fill the wontons the day of the party; cover with damp paper towels and plastic wrap and sto[ ] in the refrigerator.*

[SPI]CY CHEESE CRACKERS

[Cris]p and flaky with a touch of zip, these [crac]kers disappear fast. They're a favorite at [an]y gathering. I make them in large [qua]ntity and then freeze them so I always [hav]e some on hand.

[D]ONNA LINDECAMP MORGANTON, NC

[STA]RT TO FINISH: 30 MIN.
[MA]KES: 32 CRACKERS

- [1½] cups (6 ounces) shredded extra-sharp cheddar cheese
- [1] cup all-purpose flour
- [½] teaspoon kosher salt
- [¼] teaspoon crushed red pepper flakes
- [½] cup cold butter, cubed
- [1] to 2 tablespoons half-and-half cream

Place the cheese, flour, salt and [pep]per flakes in a food processor; [pro]cess until blended. Add butter; pulse [un]til butter is the size of peas. While [pul]sing, add just enough cream to [for]m moist crumbs.

On a lightly floured surface, roll [dou]gh to ⅛-in. thickness. Cut with a [flo]ured 3-in. holiday-shaped cookie [cut]ter. Place 2 in. apart on greased [ba]king sheets. Reroll scraps and repeat.

Bake at 350° for 13-17 minutes or [un]til golden brown. Remove from pans [to] wire racks to cool completely. Store [in] an airtight container.

LEMONY FENNEL OLIVES

The arrival of warm weather gives me spring fever. That's when I start preparing recipes with fresh flavor. This make-ahead dish can be served as an appetizer with crackers or as a garnish for a meat entree.
—**LORRAINE CALAND** SHUNIAH, ON

PREP: 20 MIN. + CHILLING
MAKES: 16 SERVINGS

- 1 small fennel bulb
- 2 cups pitted ripe olives
- 1 small lemon, cut into wedges
- ½ teaspoon whole peppercorns
- ½ cup olive oil
- ½ cup lemon juice

1. Trim fennel bulb and cut into wedges. Snip feathery fronds from fennel bulb; reserve 2 teaspoons. In a small saucepan, bring salted water to a boil. Add fennel. Boil, uncovered, for 1 minute or until crisp-tender. Drain and rinse in cold water.

2. In a large bowl, combine the fennel, olives, lemon wedges, peppercorns and reserved fennel fronds. Whisk oil and lemon juice; pour over olive mixture. Toss to coat. Cover and refrigerate overnight.

3. Remove from the refrigerator 1 hour before serving. Transfer to a serving bowl; serve with a slotted spoon.

FENNEL BULBS

Fennel is an aromatic herb and a member of the carrot family. It has a large pale green bulb, celery-like stems and feathery leaves. Fennel can be sauteed, braised or baked and added to soups, stews or salads.

COCONUT SHRIMP

PREP: 20 MIN. • **COOK:** 5 MIN./BATCH
MAKES: 6 SERVINGS

- 18 **uncooked jumbo shrimp (about 1 pound)**
- ⅓ **cup cornstarch**
- ¾ **teaspoon salt**
- ½ **teaspoon cayenne pepper**
- 3 **egg whites**
- 2 **cups flaked coconut**
  Oil for deep-fat frying

APRICOT-PINEAPPLE SALSA

- 1 **cup diced pineapple**
- ½ **cup finely chopped red onion**
- ½ **cup apricot preserves**
- ½ **cup minced fresh cilantro**
- 2 **tablespoons lime juice**
- 1 **jalapeno pepper, seeded and chopped**
  Salt and pepper to taste

1. Peel and devein shrimp, leaving t[] intact. Make a slit down inner curve [] each shrimp, starting with the tail; p[] lightly to flatten. In a shallow dish, combine the cornstarch, salt and cayenne; set aside. In a bowl, beat eg[] whites until stiff peaks form. Place th[] coconut in another shallow dish. Coa[] shrimp with cornstarch mixture; dip[] into egg whites, then coat with coco[]

2. In an electric skillet or deep-fat fryer, heat oil to 375°. Fry shrimp, a fe[] at a time, for 1 to 1½ minutes on each side or until golden brown. Drain on paper towels.

3. In a bowl, combine salsa ingredie[] Serve with shrimp.

NOTE *Wear disposable gloves when cutting hot peppers; the oils can burr[] skin. Avoid touching your face.*

> Jumbo shrimp is the perfect vehicle for crunchy, tropical coconut flakes. The fruity salsa is delightful as a dip for this island-inspired finger food.
> —**MARIE HATTRUP** SONOMA, CA

JE CHEESE-ONION
EAK BITES

pairing blue cheese with steak. Add a
garlic and onion and the flavor goes up
her notch. This is a hearty appetizer for
es or even a great light lunch.

—ELLEN NEIL ARROYO GRANDE, CA

P: 15 MIN. • **COOK:** 35 MIN.
ES: 4 DOZEN

large onions, thinly sliced into rings
tablespoons butter
garlic cloves, minced
beef tenderloin steaks
(6 ounces each)
teaspoon salt
teaspoon pepper
French bread baguette
(10½ ounces), cut into ¼-inch
slices
EAD
ounces cream cheese, softened
cup (4 ounces) crumbled blue
cheese
teaspoon salt
teaspoon pepper

1. In a large skillet, saute onions in
butter until softened. Reduce heat to
medium-low; cook, stirring
occasionally, for 30 minutes or until
onions are golden brown. Add garlic;
cook 1 minute longer.

2. Meanwhile, sprinkle beef with salt
and pepper. Using long-handled tongs,
moisten a paper towel with cooking oil
and lightly coat the grill rack.

3. Grill steaks, covered, over medium
heat or broil 4 in. from the heat for
5-7 minutes on each side or until meat
reaches desired doneness (for medium-
rare, a thermometer should read 145°;
medium, 160°; well-done, 170°). Cut
into thin slices.

4. Place bread on ungreased baking
sheets. Bake at 400° for 4-6 minutes or
until lightly browned.

5. Meanwhile, place the cream cheese,
blue cheese, salt and pepper in a food
processor; cover and process until
blended. Spread each bread slice with
1 teaspoon cheese mixture; top with
steak and onions.

Asparagus, Brie &
Parma Ham Crostini

~PARAGUS, BRIE &
~RMA HAM CROSTINI

this crostini a try if you're looking for a
~ial meal starter. Layers of asparagus
~roscuitto beneath melted Brie make
~e combo that is out of this world.

~RLA JOHNSON EAST HELENA, MT

~RT TO FINISH: 25 MIN.
~ES: 1 DOZEN

   fresh asparagus spears
   tablespoons olive oil, divided
   teaspoon salt
   teaspoon pepper
   slices French bread baguette
   (½ inch thick)
   thin slices prosciutto (Parma ham)
   or deli ham, cut into thin strips
   ounces Brie cheese, cut into
   12 slices

~ut asparagus tips into 2-in. lengths.
~card stalks or save for another use.)
~e asparagus tips in a 15x10x1-in.
~ng pan lined with foil. Drizzle with
~spoon oil and toss to coat. Sprinkle
~ salt and pepper. Bake at 425° for
~5 minutes or until crisp-tender.
~rush baguette slices on both sides
~ remaining oil. Place on a baking
~t. Broil for 1-2 minutes on each side
~ntil toasted.
~op each slice with asparagus,
~ciutto and cheese. Broil 3-4 in. from
~eat for 2-3 minutes or until cheese
~lted.

CLAMS CASINO

Your guests will be impressed with our
version of a classic upscale appetizer.
Cayenne pepper nicely seasons the bread
crumb topping.

—*TASTE OF HOME* TEST KITCHEN

PREP: 30 MIN. • **BAKE:** 15 MIN.
MAKES: 1 DOZEN

   1   **pound kosher salt**
   1   **dozen fresh cherrystone clams**
   ⅓   **cup soft bread crumbs**
   3   **tablespoons minced fresh parsley,**
       divided
   2   **tablespoons olive oil**
   1   **garlic clove, minced**
   ⅛   **teaspoon cayenne pepper**
   ⅛   **teaspoon coarsely ground pepper**

1.   Preheat oven to 450°. Spread salt
into an oven-safe metal serving platter
or a 15x10x1-in. baking pan. Shuck
clams, reserving bottom shells; drain
liquid (save for another use). Arrange
clams in salt-lined pan.
2.   Combine the soft bread crumbs,
2 tablespoons parsley, oil, garlic,
cayenne and pepper; spoon over clams.
3.   Bake 15-18 minutes or until clams
are firm and bread crumb mixture is
crisp and golden brown. Sprinkle with
remaining parsley. Serve immediately.

General Index

Alphabetical Index ·